FOOTSTEPS THROUGH
ATHINA

A TRAVELER'S GUIDE TO ATHENS AND GREEK CULTURE

ANGELYN BALODIMAS-BARTOLOMEI, PHD

Palo Albums Inc.
Park Ridge • Illinois • USA

Published by Palo Albums Inc.

Palo Albums and Palo Albums logo are trademarks of Palo Albums Inc.
Footsteps Through Athina Copyright © Palo Albums Inc. 2008. All rights reserved. No part of this publication may be reproduced or transmitted in any form or by any means, electronic or mechanical, including photocopy, recording, or any information storage and retrieval system, without written permission from Palo Albums Inc.

Palo Albums Inc. retains the copyright of the original edition of © 2009 and in all future editions, amendments and reprints.

ISBN 978-0-578-00019-0

All maps courtesy of Road Editions • www.road.gr
Photos and illustrations courtesy of Palo Albums Inc.
Some photos and illustrations courtesy of Jupitermedia Corporation
Additional photos courtesy of: Eun Mi Lee, Marianne Litgen, Maria Trakas and Sabina Trombetta
Cover layout: Melina Bartolomei
Book layout: Melina Bartolomei and Paul Bartolomei
Editors: Melina Bartolomei, Paul Bartolomei and Maria Vastis
Additional acknowledgements to: Lexy and Stephany Prodromos
Printed and bound in the United States of America

Every effort is made to provide accurate information in this publication; however, changes and new information are always taking place. Palo Albums Inc. and the author cannot accept responsibility for facts and addresses that are subject to alteration.

This book is dedicated to all whose footsteps through Athina have discovered the transcendence of this city

TABLE OF CONTENTS

PAGE

- **6** A QUICK NOTE...
- **7** INTRODUCTION
- **11** HISTORICAL TIMELINE

- **21** GETTING TO KNOW GREECE
- **33** AROUND THE ACROPOLIS

- **55** SYNTAGMA SQUARE AND SURROUNDING AREA

- **65** THE OLYMPIC AREA
- **71** PLAKA

- **97** MONASTIRAKI AND SURROUNDING AREA
- **117** THE WESTERN NEIGHBORHOODS: PSIRRI, KERAMIKOS, GAZI, THISSION

- **131** VASILISSIS SOFIAS AND KOLONAKI

UNIVERSITY AREA AND STADIOU STREET **143**

OMONIA **157**

THE OUTSKIRTS OF ATHENS **167**

2004 ATHENS OLYMPICS **173**

GREEK LANGUAGE AND EDUCATION **179**

GREEK CULTURE **195**

GREEK CUISINE **219**

SHOPPING IN ATHENS **223**

SPORTS AND LEISURE **233**

PRACTICAL INFORMATION **243**

USEFUL WEBSITES **249**

INDEX **251**

A QUICK NOTE...

Throughout this book, you will come across:

HELPFUL GREEK WORDS
η Ακρόπολη • Ee A<u>cro</u>polee • the Acropolis

These refer to the sections in which you are reading. The first set of words is the name of a place or person in Greek, followed by the English phonetic pronunciation with the accented portion underlined. Finally, the last set is the English translation.

Also for your reference, church hours will vary depending on the location and day of the week. However, they are generally open in the mornings from 9:00 am to 1:00 pm and again from 3:30 pm to 7:00 pm.

We have not listed or recommended any hotels in this publication. There are many fine hotels in Athens, covering a wide range of budgets. However, hotel prices, information and even star ratings are constantly changing. It is best to check with a travel agent or on the Internet prior to your arrival for a hotel of choice.

The same situation applies to restaurants; you will want to look around for something that suits you. It's difficult to find "bad" food in Greece, but as you walk around, you should look at the menus that are usually posted near the entrance of restaurants. This will give you an idea of the cuisine, as well as the prices. Hotel restaurants are generally more expensive than and certainly not as authentic as the local establishments.

Finally, this book goes into great detail about city sections that are primarily located in the center of Athens. Accordingly, we have provided maps for these in all our chapters. However, you may want to pick up a small, fold-out map for areas outside of the center, specifically the suburbs and outlying areas. A good map is produced by Road Editions called "Best of Athens". It's very clear, detailed, inexpensive and small enough to fit in a shirt pocket. You can find this map at most souvenir shops, book stores or kiosks.

INTRODUCTION

Dear Traveler,

Whether you are planning a trip to Athens or are just interested in learning a bit about the capital city, you are in luck - for here is an exclusive traveler's guidebook written in English about the original City of Democracy.

Throughout this book, I will take you on a tour of Athens and introduce you to its many treasures.

We will visit ancient temples dedicated to the gods of mythology, such as the great Parthenon sitting on top of the Acropolis hill, and enter museums filled with beautiful vases and statues dating back to antiquity.

We will walk around the narrow, winding paths of Plaka, the oldest neighborhood of Athens, lined with tiny, whitewashed, island type houses and Byzantine churches adorned with precious icons, mosaics and relics of saints.

INTRODUCTION

From the very beginning, you will discover that Athens is quite different from what you have probably imagined and that there is more to this city than just the distant past.

Today's Athens is very modern and cosmopolitan...

...from the newest, high-tech airport in Europe, to modern shopping malls filled with latest European fashions and excellent restaurants offering delicious Greek and international food. Athens has it all, and I have a feeling that you will quickly become as attached to this beautiful city as I am.

As you walk around, your senses will come alive!

The first thing you will notice is that Greece is a land of color and light. You will feel the brilliant Greek sunlight upon you everywhere, as it shimmers through grayish-green olive trees, and reflects upon white-washed buildings and the clear, blue, sparkling water of the Aegean Sea.

Introduction

If you are fortunate to be in Greece during the spring or summer, you will be mesmerized by the beautiful scents of blossoming trees and flowers.

You will hear the sounds of a lively, vibrant city filled with hospitable, fun loving, people eager to greet and help you.

With the help of this book, you will learn some basic Greek words and phrases. Hopefully you will give it a shot and try communicating with the locals!

(Oh, and let us not forget about the food.)

You will love the taste and smell of the delicious Greek cuisine! From neighborhood bakery shops selling hot, oven-baked bread, cookies and sweets, to outdoor tavernas serving traditional Greek meals, you need to experience it all!

INTRODUCTION

There are so many exciting things to see, do, and discover in Athens. Join me as we begin our magical journey, as our footsteps travel through this beautiful and historical city.

And as we say in Greek…

Καλώς Ορίσατε Στην Αθήνα
(Ka<u>los</u> O<u>ree</u>sate Steen A<u>thee</u>na)

"Welcome to Athens!"

Angeliki / Angie

FOOTSTEPS THROUGH ATHINA

HISTORICAL TIMELINE

	EARLY GREEK CULTURE • 3000-800 B.C.
3000 BC	Beginning of Cycladic Civilization. This period is also known as the Early Bronze Age. The Cycladic Civilization took place in the Cyclades (a group of Greek islands in the Aegean, southeast of the mainland of Greece), and is best known for its flat idols carved out of white marble from the island.
2000 BC	 Beginning of Minoan Civilization in Crete (island in the South Aegean Sea). This period is also known as the Bronze Age. The Minoan Civilization is named after the mythical king Minos who is believed to be a Minoan ruler. Many spectacular frescoes, stone carvings and pottery exist from this period of time and are displayed throughout museums of Greece. The palace of Knossos in Crete shows us that the Minoans had a plumbing and sewage system. The Minoans used a pictographic script called Linear A (which still has not been deciphered). It is believed that this civilization was destroyed by the Thera volcanic eruption that led to tsunamis; and also from invasions of Achaeans from the Peloponnesus (southwestern geographic section of mainland Greece).
1600 BC- 1100 BC	 Beginning of Mycenaean Civilization and the late Helladic Bronze Age. This name is taken from the archaeological site of Mycenae, in the northeastern Argolid region of the Peloponnesus (mainland Greece), where a great Mycenaean fortified palace once stood. Homer refers to it as the realm of King Agamemnon, leader of the Trojan War. The Mycenaeans were great warriors and engineers. They built many palaces (in Pylos, Mycenae, Tiryns, Thebes and Athens), bridges, fortification walls and buried their noble in beehive shaped tombs called *tholoi*. They produced pottery, glass and gold and bronze objects. They also used a script on tablets called Linear B to record an early Greek language. The Script was deciphered in the 20th century.

FOOTSTEPS THROUGH ATHINA

HISTORICAL TIMELINE

1400 BC	The Acropolis becomes a royal fortress.
1259 BC	Legend has it that King Theseus (a great hero from Athens) unites the province of Attica (what is today southern Greece) and founded Athens as its capital.
1200 BC	Invasions of the Dorians from northern Greece. Athens takes in refugees from the Peloponnesus.
1100-800 BC	The Dark Ages. Greece enters a period of poverty. Proto-geometric (first geometric, abstract-styled) vases are produced.

THE ARCHAIC PERIOD • 800-500 B.C.

800-600 BC	The first city-states emerge, including Athens. Kings are replaced by annually appointed 'archons' from leading families. They take up residence in Athens.
776 BC	First Olympic Games at Olympia.
750-700 BC	Homer, the legendary poet, writes the Iliad and the Odyssey.
735 BC	Greek traders exporting metals form colonies in Sicily and South Italy. This colonization has a huge cultural, linguistic and economic impact on the natives, leading to the growth of commerce and manufacture.
620 BC	Draco, the first legislator of ancient Athens, institutes harsh laws. They are extremely strict and from this, we get the word *draconian*.
594 BC	Solon (635-559), the famous Athenian lawmaker and poet, becomes archon of Athens. Slavery is abolished by property owners.

HISTORICAL TIMELINE

566 BC	First Panathenian Games (major sports competitions held every four years in Athens) begin.
560 BC	Peisistratos (605-527) becomes tyrant (sole ruler) of Athens. He promotes building and expansion and brings prosperity to Athens. Black figure pottery becomes a popular production in Athens.
508 BC	First democratic government is established in Athens. Kleisthenes, the Athenian leader, reforms the state and introduces Athenian democracy. All free men can vote. His reforms lead to the end of aristocratic rule. Athens is divided into 10 tribes. There are 50 representatives from each unit forming the council of 500.
507 BC	Athens repels attack by Sparta (strong military state of the Peloponnesus). Kleisthenes takes control of Sparta and the Spartans adopt his constitution.

THE CLASSICAL AGE • 500-337 B.C.

490 BC	First Persian War. Athenians defeat the Persians in the Battle of Marathon (Attica). The Persian Empire tries several times to invade and conquer the Greek city-states. The Persians are successful at invading, but never conquer Greece.
480 BC	The Persians under Xerxes overrun Attica. They destroy the city and the Acropolis. Athens, under Themistocles, defeats the Persian fleet at Salamis Bay (an island near Athens).
479 BC	Athens defeats Persians once again at the Battle of Plataea. Rebuilding of destructed Athens begins. Fortifications and walls enclose Piraeus.

FOOTSTEPS THROUGH ATHINA

HISTORICAL TIMELINE

461 BC	Pericles, Athens' greatest statesman, becomes Head of State. This period is known as the "The Golden Age of Pericles", as Athens witnesses its highest cultural peak in literature, art, architecture, philosophy and politics. Monumental buildings are constructed (Parthenon, Temple of Poseidon) by famous architects, such as Iktinios & Kallikrates, and adorned with sculptures by Phidias (the greatest sculptor of Classical Greece). Theaters come alive with the plays of Sophocles and Euripides. In addition, Athenians engage in the philosophy of Socrates. The voting and electoral system created form the base for all democracies today. Athens is now the hub of the Mediterranean. Greece signs a 30 year truce with Sparta and Thebes.
440 BC	Temple of Poseidon (god of the sea) is completed at Sounion (Southeastern tip of Attica).
438 BC	Phidias completes work on Parthenon.
431 BC	Beginning of the Peloponnesian War between Sparta and Athens.
429 BC	Death of Pericles.
404 BC	After years of plague, Athens is defeated by the Spartans. Peloponnesian War ends after 27 years.
387 BC	Plato founds the philosophical Academy in Athens and begins to write his philosophical works.

HISTORICAL TIMELINE

	THE HELLENISTIC PERIOD • 336-146 B.C.	
336 BC		Alexander the Great becomes king of Macedonia and begins his victorious 11 year campaign against the Persians. In addition to his conquests, he is famous for establishing city-states that were modeled on Greek institutions and for spreading Hellenism throughout the Middle East and as far as India.
330 BC	Panathenaic Stadium built by Lykourgos for the competitions of the great Panathenaia Festivities. It was originally a narrow hole in the ground.	
323 BC		Alexander the Great dies at Babylon.

	THE ROMAN EMPIRE	
146 BC	Greece becomes a Roman province. The Romans, who control Athens for some 800 years, greatly admire Greek culture and build many fine monuments during this era thanks to two great benefactors: Emperor Hadrian & Herodes Atticus.	
50 AD		Apostle Paul preaches to the Athenians in Athens on the Areopagus (Hill of Ares, northwest of the Acropolis).
124-132 AD	Temple of the Olympian Zeus finally completed. The building of the temple began in the 6th century BC but was stopped due to lack of funding.	
138 AD		The Arch of Hadrian is built around the Temple of the Olympian Zeus. The gate still bears the Roman Emperor Hadrian's name.
140 AD		Herodes Atticus restores the Panathenaic Stadium, giving it the form that was found at the 1876 excavation.
161 AD	The theater or Odeon of Herodes Atticus is built. Herodes was a wealthy Greek senator who used his money to build public projects, especially in Athens. The theater was built in honor of his wife.	
267 AD		The Goths invade and pillage Athens, but are driven out by the Romans. A makeshift wall was built around the city, leaving out several important areas such as the Agora.

Footsteps Through Athina

Historical Timeline

	THE BYZANTINE EMPIRE
330 AD	Constantine the Great, the first Christian ruler of the Roman Empire, establishes Constantinople as the capital of the Byzantine Empire. Many treasures are removed from Athens and brought to Constantinople.
395 AD	Theodosius I bans the Olympic Games. The Roman Empire is portioned. Greece becomes a part of the Byzantine Empire.
400 AD	A large gymnasium is built in the Agora to house the University of Athens.
426 AD	Christian Emperor of the East, Theodosius II, chooses to close all pagan temples. Some are converted and new Christian churches are built.
476 AD	End of Roman Empire.
529 AD	Emperor Justinian closes the Athens University and Plato's Academy, in addition to all the philosophical schools in Athens.
650 AD	The Slavs invade Greece.
1054 AD	Schism between the Church in Rome and the Church in Constantinople.
1200-1450 AD	Athens is occupied by a succession of invaders: Franks, Venetians, Catalans and Florentines.
1453 AD	Ottomans occupy Constantinople. End of Byzantium.

	OTTOMAN RULE
1456	Sultan Mehmet II conquers Athens. The Parthenon becomes a mosque. Beginning of Turkish period in Greece. Athens becomes a poor farming village.
1687	A direct hit by a Venetian cannonball destroys the Parthenon where gunpowder was stored.

1799	Britain's Lord Elgin removes the Parthenon Marbles which in the next few years would be shipped to England. To this day, there have been many campaigns to have the marbles returned to Greece.

LIBERATED GREECE • 19TH CENTURY

1821-1831	The Greek War of Independence begins. After four centuries of Turkish domination, the Greeks revolt against the Turks and eventually gain independence.
1832	King Otto (Prince of Bavaria) becomes ruler of Greece after France, Britain and Russia declare the country a Kingdom in 1831.
1834	Athens is declared the capital of Greece.
1838	The Royal Palace (today's Parliament) in Syntagma Square is completed. Bavarian architects create a city with neoclassical buildings, tree lined boulevards, flower gardens and squares.
1863	The Danish Prince George I becomes king of Greece.
1896	First Modern Olympic Games are held in Athens. 285 athletes from eleven nations compete. 43 gold medals are awarded.

20TH CENTURY GREECE

1910	Eleftherios Venizelos (a very prominent lawyer and politician) becomes Prime Minister of Greece.
1911-1913	The Balkan Wars take place. Greece wins Epirus, Macedonia, Crete and Samos.
1914-1918	World War I. Greece enters in 1917 on the side of the Allies.

Footsteps Through Athina

Historical Timeline

1916		Greece is split in two. Venizelos forms a provisional government.
1917	Venizelos assumes control of Greece.	
1920-1923		Greek-Turkish War (also called War in Asia Minor).
1923-1932		Treaty of Lausanne ends Greek-Turkish War. An exchange of populations takes place with over one million Greeks in Turkey returning to their homeland (mainly Athens and Piraeus) while 400,000 Muslims return to Turkey. Greece's population increases to 6.2 million inhabitants.
1924		King George is deposed, Greece becomes a republic. Venizelos returns to governing Greece. During this time, he institutes educational reforms and builds many primary schools. He establishes demotic Greek in the schools.
1939-1945	World War II	Greece sides with the allies.
1940		Mussolini demands access to Greek ports but Prime Minister Metaxas says "OXI" (No). The Italians invade Greece from Albania.
1941		Germany and Italy occupy Greece. 300,000 Greeks die of famine under the Germans.
1944	British troops arrive in Greece. George Papandreou, prime minister in exile, returns to Greece.	
1946-1949		Greek Civil War. More Greeks are killed in the three years of this civil war than in WWII. A quarter of a million people are left homeless and many thousands are imprisoned or exiled.

FOOTSTEPS THROUGH ATHINA

HISTORICAL TIMELINE

1947	The Dodecanese islands (group of 12 islands in the Aegean Sea) are ceded to Greece by the Italians after seven centuries of non-Greek rule over the islands.
1949	Greek Civil War ends in defeat of the Communists. Hundreds of thousands die and millions seek the safety of major cities such as Athens.
1950-1966	Prosperity returns to Greece. Constantine Karamanlis becomes prime minister in 1956, until 1964 when Papandreou takes over.
1967	Coup of Greek colonels, Junta, take over Greece. Life is very difficult at this time. Demotic Greek (the language spoken among people) is banned from Greece and replaced with Katharevousa (a formal version).
1974	Junta falls; freedom returns! The people vote for a republic, bringing back Karamanlis as prime minister.
1974-1981	Konstantine Karamanalis (Nea Demokratia-Conservatives) is leader of Greece.
1981	Greece joins the European Community, bringing the number of member states to 10. It is now called the European Union.
1981-1990	Andreas Papandreou and the socialist party rule Greece.
1990	Constantine Mitsotakis and Nea Demokratia rule Greece.
1995	Pasok under the powerful orator, Andreas Papandreou, wins election; however, he becomes ill and resigns as Prime Minister.
1996	Constantine Simitis is chosen Prime Minister.
1997	Athens is chosen as the host for the 2004 Olympics.
1999	Major earthquake in Athens causes much structural damage.

Footsteps Through Athina

HISTORICAL TIMELINE

		21ST CENTURY GREECE
	2002	First woman Athenian mayor elected; Dora Bakoyianni.
	2000-2004	Athens undergoes a complete facelift with a new airport, new train system, roads and several beautification projects.
	2004	The 2004 Athens Olympics, known as the unforgettable dream games, takes place for 17 days in Athens. Greek Soccer Team wins Euro 2004 Championships.
	2004	Kostas Karamanlis of the Nea Demokratia Party is elected as the Prime Minister of Greece.
	2006	Dora Bakoyianni becomes Minister for Foreign Affairs.
	2007	Kostas Karamanlis of the Nea Demokratia Party is reelected as the Prime Minister of Greece. Nikitas Kaklamanis is elected as Mayor of Athens.

FOOTSTEPS THROUGH ATHINA

GETTING TO KNOW GREECE

LOCATION AND SIZE

So let's get acquainted with Athens. As you already know, it is a very old city and one of the few places on earth that has a history of over 5,000 years (see Timeline for more information). During its Golden Age (5th Century BC), Athens obtained its crowning glory with architectural, artistic and intellectual achievements that deeply influenced the development of our own society. This is why Ancient Greece is generally considered to be the birthplace of Western civilization. The awesome thing about being in Athens is that you can walk atop the footpaths of the ancients where this all began. But remember, comfortable shoes are a must!

Now, let's first look at some geographical facts about the country. Greece is located at the southeastern tip of Europe and is a member of the European Union. It is bordered by the Former Yugoslavia, Albania, Bulgaria and Turkey. It is surrounded by the Aegean Sea (to the east), the Ionian Sea (to the west), and the Mediterranean Sea (to the south). It is slightly smaller than the state of Alabama. Four fifths of its land is mountainous and rocky,

Footsteps Through Athina

attributing to its sheep and goat herding production, and harvesting raisins, olives, olive oil, honey, nuts and wine. Unfortunately, Greece is limited in its greenery and trees. And since the devastating fires that occurred during the summer of 2007, much has been lost.

Athens is the largest city in Greece and also its capital. It is part of the *Nomos Attikis* (Attica-subdivision of Athens). Athens is also a seaside city and lies 5 miles (8 km) from the Bay of Phaleron, off the Aegean Sea, where its port is situated. There are many great seafood and fish tavernas along the coast. Athens is surrounded by many hills and mountains (Mt. Parnitha to the north, Mt. Pendelis to the northeast, Mt. Hymittos to the east and Mt. Aigali to west). The seasonal Kifisos River flows through western Athens, and the Illisos River crosses the eastern half.

HELPFUL GREEK WORDS

η Αθήνα • Ee Atheena • Athens
η Ελλάδα • Ee Elatha • Greece

Climate

Greece has a fabulous Mediterranean climate! Athens has plenty of sunshine (an average of 300 days of sunshine in the year. Wow... where else can you find this?). Summer months, particularly July and August, become very hot and heat waves are very common. Temperatures can reach 40 degrees Celsius (104 Fahrenheit). Be careful to take precautions with your skin to avoid sunburn. If possible, avoid the midday sun. Hats and sunglasses are advisable, as is a bottle of water and suntan lotion with a strong sun block. Many Greeks take an afternoon siesta after lunch. If you get in the habit of doing this, you will realize how beneficial it can be! And do enjoy the

Footsteps Through Athina

swimming at the many wonderful beaches around Athens (see Sports and Leisure chapter).

Winter is generally mild, sunny and warmer than most European capitals. But it does rain and can snow, as has been the case within the last few years. Since snow is unusual in Athens and the city isn't prepared for it, everything closes down when a snowfall hits. Everyone takes advantage of this rarity and dashes outside to play in the snow and build snowmen.

The best time to visit Greece is in the spring. The smell of blossoming flowers is everywhere. And also in late autumn, since it is still warm and sunny, less crowded and the prices are cheaper. The average temperature is around 19° C (66 F).

 HELPFUL GREEK WORDS

Κάνει ζέστη • <u>Ka</u>nee <u>zes</u>tee • it is hot
Κάνει κρύο • <u>Ka</u>nee <u>kree</u>o • it is cold
Χιονίζει • Hio<u>nee</u>zee • It is snowing
Βρέχει • <u>Vre</u>hee • It is raining

Time

Greece operates on Eastern European time which is two hours ahead of Greenwich Mean Time. The following chart shows the difference between Greece and other time zones.

Los Angeles USA	New York USA	London England	Athens Greece	Sydney Australia
9 am	12 pm	5 pm	7 pm	3 am

 HELPFUL GREEK WORDS

Τι ώρα είναι • Tee <u>o</u>ra <u>ee</u>ne • What time is it?
Είναι δύο η ώρα • <u>Ee</u>nay <u>dee</u>o ee <u>o</u>ra • It is two o'clock.

FOOTSTEPS THROUGH ATHINA

POPULATION & PEOPLE

When Athens became the capital in 1834, it was a very small town with no more than 124,000 inhabitants. Today the city of Athens is very overpopulated. According to the 2001 census report, 3,192,606 million people live in this city. This is over a third of the total population of Greece. You will need to adjust to the rhythm of this vibrant city: traffic, drivers honking their horns, crowded streets and sidewalks with a lot of noise. But don't worry; Greeks are fun-loving people. They enjoy talking, walking and having a great time. You will see that they go out to eat rather late (kids too!) and often go for a walk after dinner. After a short time there, you too will soon be acting like them and taking part in everyday activities. So when in Greece, do as the Greeks do (and me, too!)...enjoy every moment! "OPA!"

Many of the residents of Athens are newcomers who migrated from other parts of Greece, Asia Minor, or from Greek communities in other countries. Until quite recently, most of the residents were Greek except for a small minority of Turks, Slavs, Vlachs, Pomaks, Bulgarians, Armenians and gypsies. Since the 1980's, Athens has become a host country to large numbers of migrants and is now home to many people from the former Soviet Union, Bangladesh, Iran, Iraq and the Philippines. You will notice many ethnic restaurants and hear a variety of foreign languages spoken when walking around the neighborhoods of downtown Athens where many immigrants live.

HELPFUL GREEK WORDS

Δεν μιλάω ελληνικά • Den mee<u>la</u>o elleenee<u>ka</u> • I don't speak Greek.
Μιλάτε αγγλικά • Mee<u>la</u>tay angleeka • Do you speak English?
Μιλάω αγγλικά • Mee<u>la</u>o angleeka • I speak English
Απο που είσαι • A<u>po</u> pou <u>ee</u>se? • Where are you from?
Είμαι από την Αμερική • <u>Ee</u>me a<u>po</u> teen Ameree<u>kee</u> • I am from America.

FOOTSTEPS THROUGH ATHINA

CURRENCY

As of January 2002, the Euro (pronounced *evro* in Greek) is the currency of Greece. It replaced the Drachma that was the national currency of Greece since 1833. Currently, fifteen European Union countries have adopted the Euro. Every Euro coin carries a common European face: however, each country has decorated its own motifs on one side of the coins. There are eight coins denominated in 2 and 1 Euros and then 50, 20, 10, 5, 2 and 1 cent. They range in size and color.

2 EURO

This gold coin trimmed with silver illustrates a mythological scene from a 3rd century BC mosaic in Sparta. It features the goddess Europa being abducted by Zeus who has taken the shape of a bull.

1 EURO

This coin is silver with a gold trim. It was designed from an ancient Athenian 4 drachma coin from the 5th century BC and illustrates an owl, which is the symbol of wisdom.

50 CENT EURO

This gold coin illustrates Eleftherios Venizelos (1896-1936), one of Greece's most important political figures. He was a pioneer in social reform and played a prominent role in modernizing the Greek state and liberating Northern Greece and the Aegean Islands. The new airport is also named after him.

20 CENT EURO

The 20 cent gold Euro coin commemorates Ioannis Kapodistrias (1776-1831), the first governor of Greece after the War of Independence (1821-

25

FOOTSTEPS THROUGH ATHINA

1827). He made many notable contributions to domestic policy, education, justice, public works, social welfare, agriculture, stock breeding, trade and shipping.

10 CENT EURO

This gold coin features Rigas Velestinlis-Fereos (1757-1798). He was a forerunner and leading figure of the Greek Enlightenment and a visionary of the Balkan liberation from the Ottoman rule.

5 CENT EURO

This bronze coin displays a modern tanker ship reflecting the innovative spirits of Greek shipping which is still today a major part of Greece's economy.

2 CENT EURO

The two cent bronze Euro coin illustrates a Corvette, a type of ship used during the Greek War of Independence (1821).

1 CENT EURO

This bronze coin illustrates an advanced model of an Athenian Trireme, the largest warship afloat for more than 200 years, dating from the time of Athenian Democracy (5th century BC). It is the smallest sized coin in the Euro collection.

There are seven Euro banknotes in different colors and sizes. They are denominated in 5, 10, 20, 50, 100, 200 and 500 Euros. Unlike the coins, the Euros are uniform and have no national side. The designs are symbolic for Europe's architectural heritage and do not represent any existing monuments.

HELPFUL GREEK WORDS

Πόσο κάνει • Poso kanee • How much is it?

FOOTSTEPS THROUGH ATHINA

LANGUAGE ΑΒΓΔ

The Greek language is the official language of Greece. It is a very old language (over 3,000 years old). The Greek Alphabet has been a written alphabet since the 9th century BC, making it the oldest alphabet script that is still used today. It was the first alphabet that had a symbol for both vowels and consonants. Modern Greek derives from the same language used by the ancient poet, Homer. The Greek alphabet and language have influenced all European languages. Many of our English (especially scientific and medical) words are derived from it. Today, the letters are used for mathematical symbols, particle names in physics, names of stars, tropical cyclones and also for fraternities and sororities.

There are 24 letters in the Greek alphabet. Several of these letters are the same ones that we use in the English alphabet. Learning to read the alphabet will help you read signs and menus. It is also good to learn some Greek words. Greeks are happy when you try to speak their language. But not to worry... many Greeks speak English. In fact, Greece is rated the #1 country in the European Union for knowing and speaking the most foreign languages.

RELIGION

About 98% of the Greek population belongs to the Greek Orthodox Church. The majority of the other 2% are Muslim, Roman Catholic and Jewish. The Orthodox Church plays an important part in Greek people's lives. Ceremonies such as weddings, baptisms, funerals and church feast days are spent by attending church, then gathering together with family and friends to eat and observe the occasion. Several holy days are national holidays in Greece.

Greek churches are very elaborate and filled with beautiful religious icons (flat paintings depicting a holy being or object such as Jesus, Mary, the saints, angels or a cross) on the walls, ceiling

27

Footsteps Through Athina

and around the holy altar. When Greek people enter the narthex (entrance) of the church they immediately light a candle, make the sign of the cross and then kiss the religious icon. Some of the smaller churches do not have pews. There are a few seats reserved for elderly people (or those in need of a seat) at the sides of the church. The liturgy (church service) can be very long, but the services are very festive. Greek priests dress in ornate vestments, the chanters sing Byzantine hymns and the priest uses incense.

Most Greek churches can be recognized by their big dome. Inside of this dome, there is almost always a large painting of Christ in Judgment (Pantokratora) looking down at you. It is symbolic of a window to the spiritual world. The architecture and style of the church will differ depending on when and where it was built. On the islands, many of the churches are blue and white. You can even see these along the coast of Athens. Greece has many old churches dating back to the Byzantine times. These too will look different than some of the newer churches. You will notice that the arrangement and colors of the bricks differ. Byzantine and Neo-Byzantine churches are built in a cross shape and square plan; the church is cubical on the first level and in a form of the cross on the second level. The dome rests on a cylinder at the intersection of the arms of the cross.

Churches tend to be very small in villages and much bigger in Athens. It has the highest concentration of Byzantine churches built during the late Byzantine period. The Cathedral of Athens can be found here and we will visit this beautiful church as we walk around the city.

HELPFUL GREEK WORDS

η εκκλησία • Ee ekle<u>ee</u>s<u>ee</u>a • the church
Ο παπάς • O pa<u>pas</u> • the priest
Ο σταυρός • O stav<u>ros</u> • the cross

ARCHAEOLOGICAL SITES AND GREEK COLUMNS

DORIC   IONIC   CORINTHIAN

The Ancient Greeks strived for perfection in the appearance of their temples. Greek architecture was based on a highly structured system of proportion, symmetry and unity. This system was developed according to three styles, or orders: Doric, Ionic, and Corinthian. Each order consists of an upright support called a column that extends from the base to a shaft in the middle, to the top which is called a capital (see diagram on next page).

As you walk around the many temples in Athens, you will notice that the columns, bases and tops of the monuments vary in their form of architecture. It is necessary to understand the different types of architectural differences.

DORIC: This style is the oldest and simplest of the three orders. It is characterized by heavy fluted columns and plain capitals. There is no base in the Doric order. The Parthenon and the Hephaisteion are built in the Doric style.

IONIC: The Ionic order is characterized by two opposed volutes (scroll-like ornaments) in the capital. It is called Ionic because it was developed in Ionia (the southwestern coastland and islands of Asia Minor) in the 6th century B.C. The Ionic shafts (columns) are taller than the Doric columns and make the columns look slender. The shafts have a characteristic called entasis (to strain); this means that they have a little bulge in the columns that make them look straight from a distance. The base of the Ionic temple is large and looks like a stack of rings. The Temple of Nike is the only building in Athens completely built in Ionic order. The Propylaia and the Erechtheion incorporate Ionic order structures.

Footsteps Through Athina

CORINTHIAN: The Corinthian order is the most ornate of the three orders. Although it was designed by the Greeks, it seldom was used in Greek architecture as temples with this style were mainly built in Ancient Rome. It is named after the city of Corinth and characterized by a slender fluted column having an ornate bell-shaped capital decorated with acanthus leaves. The Corinthian column also uses the entasis characteristic to make it look straight. The base is like the Ionic base; it is large and resembles a stack of rings.

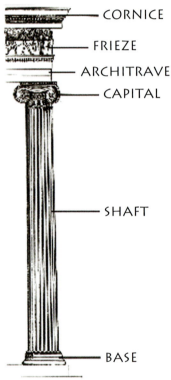

- CORNICE
- FRIEZE
- ARCHITRAVE
- CAPITAL
- SHAFT
- BASE

HELPFUL GREEK WORDS

Δωρικός • Doree<u>kos</u> • Doric
Ιωνικός • Eoonee<u>kos</u> • Ionic
Κορινθιακός • Koreenthee<u>akos</u> • Corinthian

FOOTSTEPS THROUGH ATHINA

ATHENS MAP

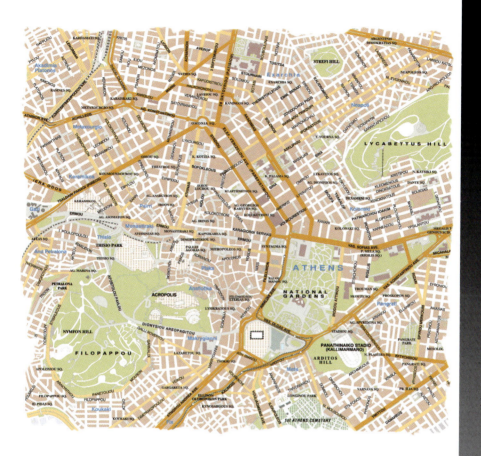

GETTING TO KNOW GREECE

Footsteps Through Athina

Athens Metro

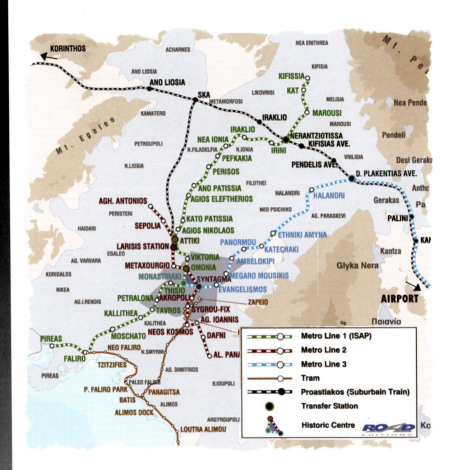

FOOTSTEPS THROUGH THE ACROPOLIS

Oh, the awesome Acropolis that overlooks the city of Athens! It doesn't matter how many photos you have seen of this magnificent landmark; there is nothing like visiting it in person. This mammoth, steep-sided limestone made rock is the number one destination for tourists (and me, too!) to visit in Greece. You will want to visit it shortly after your arrival in Athens.

The Acropolis Hill, meaning "high city" in Greek or "Sacred Rock" as it is often called, is the most important site in Athens. Early artifacts and archaeology show us that the first remains of habitation on the Acropolis date back to the Neolithic period (7000-3000 BC). It became a fortified citadel in the Mycenaean period (13th century BC). Over the centuries, the "Sacred Rock" was used both as a residential area for kings and a place of worship. In 480 BC the Persians destroyed all of the previous buildings on the Acropolis during the Persian War. Soon after, Pericles set out to rebuild Athens and make it the most beautiful city in the world. The Acropolis was among his many projects.

New marble temples and bronze or painted statues appeared high on the Acropolis giving it quite a different look than it has today. These splendid works were designed by the sculptor Phidias and the architects, Iktinos and Kallikrates. They used the principles of geometry and optics to build the temples. The second half of the 5th century BC became known as the Golden Age of

Footsteps Through Athina

Greece, a period when the most beautiful art and architecture, philosophy and literature evolved. Pericles transformed the Acropolis into a city of temples which became regarded as the zenith of classical Greek achievement. The most important monuments on the Acropolis and the same ones that we see today are: the Parthenon, the Erechtheion, the Temple of Athena Nike and the Propylaia.

The Entrance to the Acropolis

The main entrance to the Acropolis is on the western side and there are a few approaches to reaching this point. The most common way is take the Pedestrian Walk (this will be discussed later in this chapter) west to the junction of Dionysiou Areopagitou & Rovertou Galli.

If you are in western Plaka, you can follow a street

Footsteps Through Athina

called Dioskouron that meets Theorias street. Take Theorias street southwest until you reach the main entrance.

You will notice a booth selling tickets and a sign pointing to the Theater. Don't forget to get a ticket for 12 Euros that is valid for four days and can be used on multiple sites. Just be sure to wear comfortable shoes for there are many slippery steps in your approach. There are a few stands selling water, soft drinks and snacks. If you forget to bring your water, you might want to pick some up here since there are no shops or restaurants on the Acropolis. Keep in mind however that the snack shop prices are high!

After climbing a long series of steps you can enter the Acropolis by passing through the Beule Gate (it is named after the 19th century French archaeologist who discovered it). The gate was built in 280 BC of material from the choragic monument of Nikias and other structures. Admission tickets are also sold here.

Throughout the centuries, earthquakes, fires, vandalism and pollution have led to the deterioration of the Acropolis. As a result, the majority of the temples have been undergoing reconstruction for the past several years. Keep in mind that there are many scaffolds on the hill.

FOOTSTEPS THROUGH ATHINA

THE PROPYLAIA

You are about to enter the Acropolis. Follow the large Roman built steps up to the Propylaia of the Acropolis; the grandest entranceway ever built in the classical Hellenic world. Designed by the architect Mnesikles and constructed in 437-432 BC, this Pentelic marble monument dedicated to the goddess Athena is more like a temple than an entrance area.

The Propylaia consists of a central hall, with two Doric porticoes (wings) on each side. Each section had a gate and in ancient times the existing five gates were the only entrances to the upper city. The western portico of the Propylaia consisted of rows of Ionic and Doric columns and a vestibule with a blue painted ceiling decorated with gold stars. The north wing was used as a pinakothiki (a picture gallery) and the south wing was the antechamber to the Temple of Athena Nike.

FOOTSTEPS THROUGH ATHINA

TEMPLE OF ATHENA NIKE

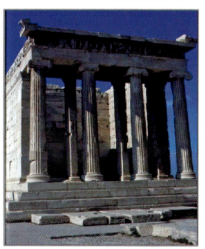

The first temple that you normally see when visiting the Acropolis is the Temple of Athena Nike (*nike* means "victory" in Greek). It has undergone many reconstructions and unfortunately, since 2002, it was removed altogether to be repaired off site and is still absent from this spot. Here is a description of what you would normally see if it was in place:

The temple sits on a platform at the right hand side of the Propylaia and overlooks the Saronic Gulf (arm of the Aegean Sea in southern Greece between Attica and the Peloponnese east of Corinth). It was constructed in 427-424 BC by the architect Kallikrates and built of Pentelic Marble from the Penteli Mountain (a tall mountain in the northern suburbs of Athens). The building is almost square, with four graceful Ionic columns at both ends. It is the only temple on the Acropolis that is completely Ionic.

The temple is much different today than when it was built. Originally it contained friezes that consisted of mythological (a meeting with the gods Athena, Zeus, and Poseidon) and historical scenes (victory of the Persians at the battle of Plataea). The platform was surrounded by relief sculptures, some of which are now in the Acropolis museum. The temple also housed a statue of the goddess Athena without wings. The wings were removed by the Athenians in hope that she would remain in Athens and protect the city from the Spartans. In 1686, the Turks dismantled the temple for fortifications and placed a large cannon on its platform. In 1835 (after the Greek War of Independence) the temple was placed in its original position. However, since then it has been dismantled a few times for reconstruction.

The Parthenon
Focal Point of the Acropolis

You are finally here in front of the breathtaking Parthenon, also known as the Temple of Athena. It is the most famous surviving building of ancient Greek civilization and one of the most renowned edifices in the world. The Parthenon, dedicated to the city's patron goddess Athena Parthenos (the virgin) has stood atop the Acropolis for nearly 2,500 years. It was built between 447 and 438 BC (Golden Age of Greece). The construction of the Parthenon was initiated by Pericles, and Iktinos and Kallikrates were the architects of the building. Its decorative sculptures were completed in 432 BC by the famous Athenian sculptor, Phidias. It was the first building on mainland Greece to have been built completely of marble. Financial records have shown us that the cost of the Parthenon was very high, especially for transporting its marble from Mount Pentelikos (about 16 km from Athens).

The Parthenon is built in the Doric order. There are eight columns on each of the narrow sides and seventeen columns on each of the long ones. These columns appear straight however they were expertly sculptured by Iktinos and actually become thinner from the middle up creating an optical illusion called *entasis*. For many centuries, there was an immense, forty foot, gold and ivory statue of Athena (made by Phidias), inside the Cella (central part of the temple). During the 5th century AD, the statue was looted, taken to Constantinople and later destroyed. Today, you can no longer enter and walk inside the Cella. At one time, the Parthenon was very colorful (red, blue, green), however throughout the ages, sand, sun and pollution have caused the colors to fade.

The Parthenon was not always used as a temple. In the 6th AD century, it was converted into a Christian Church. When Athens fell to the Ottomans in 1456, the Parthenon was converted into a mosque and a minaret was added. Throughout these  conversions, the internal columns and some of the walls of the Cella were removed.

Although the temple survived for many centuries, it has suffered great damage throughout the ages. As a result, the Parthenon has been undergoing reconstruction for several years. In 1687, the temple was used by the Turks as ammunition depot where weapons and gunpowder were stored. The central part of the Parthenon was destroyed during a Venetian siege when a cannonball hit the temple and the gunpowder exploded. In 1801, most of the surviving sculptures (friezes, metopes, columns and one caryatid from the Erechtheion) were removed by Lord Elgin and sold to the British government. Ever since, they have been on display in the British Museum in London. For several years, the Greek government, along with the determination, optimism, and dedication of the late Melina Mercouri, has fought to have these marbles returned permanently to Greece and now… the new Acropolis Museum stands ready to welcome back their masterpieces.

The Erechtheion

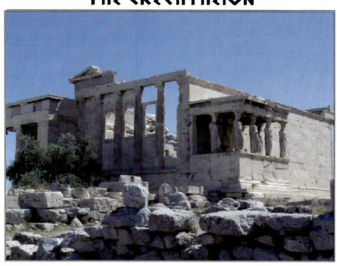

The Erechtheion is situated on the northern part of the Acropolis and was built between 421 and 406 BC. The temple takes its name from Poseidon Erechtheus, the mythical king of Attica, and was a sanctuary to both Athena Polias and Erechtheus (Poseidon).

This extraordinary Ionic order monument was built in different levels and consists of three basic parts: the main temple, the northern porch and southern porch. The main temple is divided into two cellae (central parts), one dedicated to Athena and the other to Poseidon. Athena's cell contained the holy olive wood statue of Athena Pallas. The northern porch consists of six beautiful ionic columns. It is believed that this is where Poseidon struck the ground with his trident, making a fountain of pure water spring up. This porch leads to the spot where Athena's olive tree 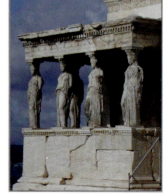 sprouted in their battle for possession of the city. The southern porch is that of the Caryatids, the maiden statues in Ionic tunics. They are called Caryatids because the women who modeled for the

FOOTSTEPS THROUGH ATHINA

statues were from Karyes in Laconia. Due to pollution, the maiden statues have been replaced with plaster casts. The original maidens are exhibited in the new Acropolis Museum.

INFORMATION:

Summer Hours: The Acropolis is open from 8:00 am to 6:30 pm every day; however these hours can change, so make sure that you check ahead of time. Sometimes it is open during the evening of the full moon in the summer.

Cost of entrance: About 12 Euros - this ticket is also valid for 4 days upon purchase for other sites in the area: Ancient Agora, Theater of Dionysos, Keramikos, Roman Agora, Tower of the Winds and the Temple of Olympian Zeus. You can also buy individual tickets to these sites.

Directions to the Acropolis: Metro Stop Acropolis; or from the Northwest side of Plaka; or from Syntagma Square take Amalias Street to the large pedestrian street Dionysiou Areopagitou that starts near Hadrian's Arch. Follow the marble paths that lead up the hill.

Additional Tips: No backpacks or big sacks are allowed (these will have to be checked in so it's best not to bring them). Don't forget to stock up on bottled water. It gets very hot on the Acropolis. Plan to spend a few hours here. There is so much to see. Find a quiet spot to sit and take in all the magnificent monuments. And don't forget your camera!

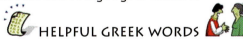

HELPFUL GREEK WORDS

η Ακρόπολη • Ee A<u>cro</u>polee • the Acropolis

Που είναι η είσοδος για την Ακρόπολη • Poo <u>ee</u>nay ee <u>ee</u>sodos yia teen A<u>cro</u>polee? • Where is the entrance for the Acropolis?

Τα Προπύλαια • Ta Pro<u>pee</u>lea • The Propylaia

Ο Ναός της Αθηνάς Νίκης • O Na<u>os</u> tees Athee<u>nas</u> <u>Nee</u>kees • The Temple of Athena Nike

Ο Παρθενώνας • O Parthe<u>non</u>as • The Parthenon

Το Ερέχθειο • To E<u>rech</u>theeo • The Erechtheion

AROUND THE ACROPOLIS

FOOTSTEPS THROUGH ATHINA

Footsteps Under the Acropolis

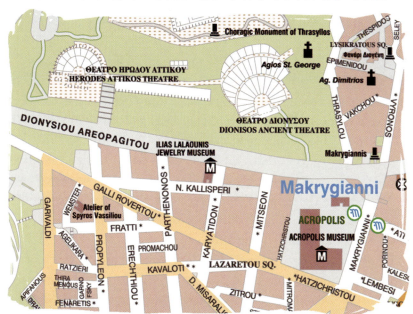

Odeon and Theater of Herod Atticus

The theater of Herod Atticus is on the southern slope, under the Acropolis, on Dionysiou Aeropagitou Street. It was built in 160 AD by the Roman governor Atticus in memory of his wife, Regilla. It is a typical example of a classic Roman style Odeon (theater for musical performances) with big arches providing both support and beauty. It seats approximately five thousand spectators in rows of beautiful marble seats. The front row consists of marble thrones for VIPs (very important people). The interior has been restored and the theater is now used for the annual summer Athens Festival where you can enjoy music recitals, ancient drama, concerts, ballet, and other performances by some of the top orchestras and troupes of the world. Try to attend a performance - you won't be disappointed. Just a reminder... in an effort to prevent damage to this site, cell phones, water, food, chewing gum and high heels have been banned from the theater.

Theater of Dionysos

The Theater of Dionysos (dedicated to the god of theater and wine) is at the southern slope of the Acropolis. Built in the 5th century BC, it was the world's first stone theater ever built and the birthplace of Greek tragedy. People came to see the plays of Aeschylus, Sophocles, Euripides and Aristophanes. It was here that the Dionysia Festival took place. This festival included drama contests.

The theater was built in several stages. Each stage corresponded with the developments of drama. The front row seats, decorated with satyrs and lions, were reserved for the priests of Dionysos. During the Roman period, the theater was used as an arena and could seat as many as 17 thousand people. What we see today are the remains of that period.

INFORMATION
Admission Cost: About 12 Euros (Acropolis ticket is valid here)
Summer Hours: 8:00 am - 7:30 pm

FOOTSTEPS THROUGH ATHINA

AROUND THE ACROPOLIS

CHORAGIC MONUMENT OF THRASYLLOS

The Choragic Monument of Thrasyllos was built in 319 BC. It is situated above the Theater of Dionysos, under the Acropolis. The monument was established to commemorate the victory of Thrasyllos' drama competition. Today it serves as the chapel of the Panagia Spiliotissa Church.

AGIOS GEORGIOS · ST. GEORGE

St. George of Alexandria is a very small church that it located east of the Theater of Dionysos. In contrast with its size, it maintains a great significance in Greek history. In 1826, the Turks were fighting to regain control of the Acropolis. The Greeks realized that in order to win and inflict major casualties on their enemies, they needed to sacrifice this church. So, they placed explosives in this tiny church and as the Turks swarmed around it, two men, Michaelis Kounelis and Thomas Argyrokastris lit the fuse. The Turks were defeated, but unfortunately the church fell in ruins. It was rebuilt afterwards on the same site.

 **HELPFUL GREEK WORDS**

Το Ωδείο του Ηρώδου • To O<u>dee</u>io tou E<u>er</u>othou • The Theater of Herod

Το Θέατρο του Διονύσου • To <u>Theatro</u> tou Deeo<u>nee</u>sou • The Theater of Dionysos

Το χορηγικό μνημείο του Θρασύλλου • To choreeyee<u>ko</u> mnee<u>mee</u>o tou Thra<u>see</u>lou • The Choragic Monument of Thrasyllos

Ο ΄Αγιος Γεώργιος • O <u>A</u>yeeos <u>Yior</u>geeos • Agios Georgios - St. George

FOOTSTEPS THROUGH ATHINA

PEDESTRIAN WALK
ARCHAEOLOGICAL PARK

For decades, archaeologists and city planners dreamt about linking the sites of the historic center together. And shortly before the Athens 2004 Olympics, this dream became a reality. The newly constructed pedestrian walk, or Archaeological Park, borders the south and west slopes of the Acropolis. The giant pedestrian walkways take you to several of the archaeological sites. Dionysiou Areopagitou street leads from Hadrian's Gate to the south side of the Acropolis and around the district of Makrygianni.

Lined with cafes, restaurants and restored neoclassical buildings, the walkways have become a favorite place for Athenians to take their evening strolls, and for children to ride bikes and play soccer. You too can walk around the scenic routes enjoying the views of the Acropolis (it is awesome to see it lit at night) and other archaeological sites, while listening to the various musicians performing either in the Herod Theater or along the walks.

The Acropolis Metro Station

The Acropolis Metro Station is located at the foothills of the Acropolis, in the Makrygianni Area. It has two entrances and exits at Makrygianni and Ath. Diakou. Unlike most train stations, the three leveled Acropolis Metro Station is more like a museum than a train station. It is filled with exhibitions displaying the actual archaeological findings from the excavations (when the station was being built), along with reproductions from the Parthenon. The lower level from where the trains pass is dedicated to Melina Mercouri, the famous actress and Minister of Culture who fought to have the Elgin Parthenon Marbles returned to Athens. The Greek government is still in the process of trying to bring them back to Greece.

FOOTSTEPS THROUGH ATHINA

THE ACROPOLIS MUSEUM
Odos (street): 2-4 Makrygianni

The Acropolis Museum was originally located on the Acropolis hill, east of the Parthenon. Considered one of the most important museums in the world, it housed the masterpieces from the Acropolis and Archaic world.

The old museum closed down for a very good reason: it was too small to exhibit all of the antiquities. A new, state-of-the-art

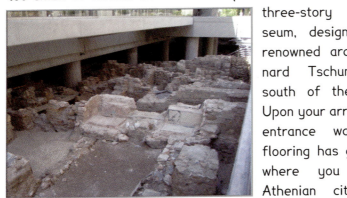

three-story glass museum, designed by the renowned architect, Bernard Tschumi, opened south of the Acropolis. Upon your arrival past the entrance walkway, the flooring has glass panels where you can view Athenian city remains, dating back from pre-historic times to the Byzantine period. These glass panels are also found inside throughout the first floor.

Natural light is the design emphasis for the museum. Glass wall and ceiling panels provide a display in which the visitor can view the works of art as if they were in their original outdoors settings. From the 3rd floor, visitors are able to view the Acropolis.

AROUND THE ACROPOLIS

47

FOOTSTEPS THROUGH ATHINA

The museum exhibits priceless works of art from the Archaic, Classical, Post Parthenon, Roman and Byzantine eras. The majority of these were all found on or around the Acropolis. Up until the museum opening, works of art were either scattered among other Greek and foreign museums or held in storage. Now visitors have the opportunity to view all works in historical sequence.

One of the main attractions here is a solid concrete core that exhibits the Parthenon frieze as it was in its original location on the temple. The museum planners also allocated space for the missing friezes that are housed in the British museum in London. Many of these missing pieces were sold to the British Museum by Lord Elgin in the 19th century. The Greek government is making every attempt to bring the marbles back home to be exhibited here.

AROUND THE ACROPOLIS

48

FOOTSTEPS THROUGH ATHINA

DISTRICT OF MAKRYGIANNI

The district of Makrygianni is located next to Dionysiou Areopagitou Street on the Pedestrian Walk. It was named after General Ioannis Makrygiannis, a war hero from the 19th century who lived in this neighborhood. In addition to fighting for his country, he later donated part of his property for the creation of Zappeion Gardens. His statue can be seen on this street.

Makrygianni is a very old residential area of Athens with beautiful neoclassical and art deco buildings. In fact, there has been quite a controversy over demolishing a few very famous landmarks in preparation for the new Acropolis museum. One of those buildings belongs to the famous composer, Vangelis Papathanassiou who won the Oscar for his song "Chariots of Fire". His building  consists of beautiful carved statues and mosaics which have been considered national monuments since 1978. Today, this neighborhood has become quite upscale and trendy with the development of interesting museums, shops, restaurants, hotels and clubs.

ATELIER OF SPYROS VASSILIOU

Odos: 5A Wemster Street
Hours: Tues - Thurs - Fri: 10.00 am – 6:00 pm
Wednesday: 11:00 am – 8:00 pm
Saturday – Sunday: 10:00 am – 3:00 pm

Spyros Vassiliou (1902-1985) was a famous Greek painter who was inspired by Greek neighborhoods and simple people. His paintings reflected his passion for simplicity in a surreal manner. Since he lived across the

FOOTSTEPS THROUGH ATHINA

street from the Parthenon, he often used this monument as a background for his paintings. In 2004, his house became a museum/workshop open to the public. Upon visiting it, you can familiarize yourself with his interesting and wonderful works.

ILIAS LALAOUNIS JEWELRY MUSEUM

Odos: 2 Karyatidon
Hours: Monday – Thursday – Friday – Saturday: 9:00 am - 4:00 pm
Wednesday: 9.00 am - 9:00 pm
Sunday: 11:00 am – 4: 00 pm

The Ilias Lalaounis Museum is the only jewelry museum in Greece. It opened in 1994 and today houses over 4,000 pieces of jewelry and mini sculptures designed by the owner, Ilias Lalaounis. Ilias, a fourth generation jeweler, is renowned for his creations that are inspired from the historical past, such as the Neolithic, Mycenaean, Byzantine and Pre-Columbian Eras. His pricey jewelry shops can be found throughout the world.

HELPFUL GREEK WORDS

Η Διονυσίου Αρεοπαγίτου • Ee Deeonee<u>see</u>ou Areopa<u>gee</u>too • Dionysiou Areopagitou

Που είναι ο σταθμός για το μετρό • Poo <u>ee</u>ne o stath<u>mos</u> yea to Me<u>tro</u>? • Where is the Metro station?

Ο Σταθμός Ακρόπολης • O stath<u>mos</u> A<u>cro</u>polees • Acropolis Station

Το μουσείο της Ακρόπολης • To mou<u>see</u>io tees A<u>cro</u>polees • The Acropolis Museum

Το άγαλμα του Μακρυγιάννη • To <u>a</u>galma tou Makree<u>yia</u>nee • The statue of Makrygianni

Ο Σπύρος Βασιλείου • O <u>Spee</u>ros Vasee<u>lee</u>ou • Spyros Vassiliou

Ο καλλιτέχνης • O kalee<u>tech</u>nees • The artist

Το κοσμηματοπωλείο • To kosmeematopo<u>leeo</u> • The jewelry shop

FOOTSTEPS THROUGH ATHINA

FOOTSTEPS AROUND THE HILLS OF THE ACROPOLIS

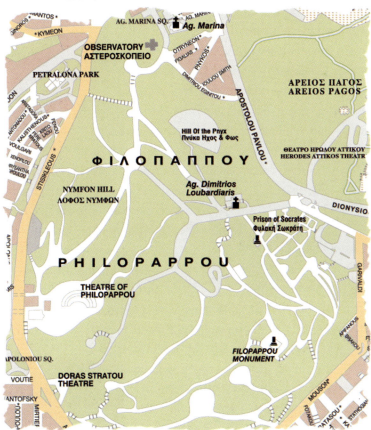

AREOS PAGOS

There are four historical hills located west of the Acropolis. Areos Pagos (also called the hill of Ares or Mars) is across from the entrance of the Acropolis on Dionysiou Areopagitou Avenue. It is often referred to as the Hill of Justice since it served as the seat of the court in classical times. During the Roman period, Apostle Paul preached to the Athenians on this very spot. The hill has very slippery marble stairs and the climb is difficult, so be sure to wear very comfortable shoes when visiting this site.

Pnyx Hill

Further west is Pnyx Hill, the birthplace of democracy. It is a small hill surrounded by park land and a large platform of eroded stone set into its side. During the 5th century BC, this was the meeting place of the Public Assembly (Ekklesia) where the Athenians gathered to debate and govern the state of Athens. Many great orators such as Pericles,  Aristides, and Demosthenes gave their speeches here. Today it serves as the site of the Sound and Light Show of the Acropolis, running each night from April to October: an event worth seeing!

 There is also a small Byzantine church on this hill: Saint Dimitrios the Bombardier or Loumbardiaris. In 1645, Yusuf Aga, a Turkish commander, planned to massacre all of the Christians at this church on the feast day of St. Dimitrios. He closed all the neighboring churches so that everyone would be forced to go to this church that he had planned to bomb. But he did not succeed. The night before, there was a terrible storm and lightening hit the gunpowder that was stored in the Propylaia of the Acropolis. Aga and his  family were killed and the Greeks were saved. Close to the church, you will notice a cave in the rock. This is what is popularly known as Socrates prison.

Information for Sound & Light Show on Pnyx Hill:
Performances in English on Monday, Wednesday, Thursday, Saturday and Sunday – April to October
Time: 9:00 pm
Ticket can be purchased at the Hellenic Festival Office - 39 Panepistimiou or at the entrance of the Sound & Light Show.

Nymphs Hill

Nymphs Hill is located southwest of the Pnyx Hill. The hill was famous in ancient times because this is where the nymphs were worshipped. In 1842, the National Observatory was built on this hill. It was the first research institution to be constructed after the fall of the Ottoman Empire. Today it operates five research institutes, a library and also includes an astro-geophysics museum that houses clocks, telescopes, and other instruments from the 19th century. The impressive church of St. Marina (patron saint of childbirth) is near the observatory. It was built in 1922, on the site of an older, 19th century church. Southeast of the church there is a small Byzantine church carved into the rock. This church is also dedicated to St. Marina.

Philopappou Hill

Philopappou is the tallest of these hills. In ancient times, the hill was dedicated to the Nine Muses, the goddesses of arts and science. It was later named after the Roman monarch from Syria, Gaius Julius Antiochus Philoppapos who was a great benefactor to the city of Athens. In the 2nd century AD, the Philoppapos Monument (a marble tower) was built in his memory. This is a great spot to take photos since you are almost eye level with the Acropolis. It is also

FOOTSTEPS THROUGH ATHINA

home to the Dora Stratou Folkdance Theater in which 75 dancers, musicians and folk singers perform in beautiful, authentic costumes representing 2,500 villages of Greece. Be sure to squeeze this into your schedule!

Information for Dora Stratou Folkdance Performances:
May through October
Tuesday - Saturday: 9:30 pm
Sunday: 8:15 pm - Mondays: closed
You can buy tickets at the box office, Odos Scholio 8 in the Plaka, from 8:00am to 2:00pm Tel: 01/924-4395, or 01/921-4650 after 5:30pm. Tickets are also usually available at the theater before performances.

 HELPFUL GREEK WORDS

Ο Άρειος Πάγος • O Areeos Pagos • Areos Pagos
Ο λόφος της Πνύκας • O lofos tees Pneekas • Pnyx Hill
Το Ήχος και Φως • To eehos ke fos • Sound and Light
Ο λόφος των Νυμφών • O lofos ton neemfon • Nymphs Hill
Ο λόφος του Φιλοπάππου • O lofos tou Feelopapou • Philopappou Hill
Οι Ελληνικοί χοροί • Ee elleeneekee horee • Greek dances
Το Θέατρο της Δώρας Στράτου • To Theatro tees Thoras Stratou • The Theater of Dora Stratou

FOOTSTEPS THROUGH SYNTAGMA SQUARE AND SURROUNDING AREA

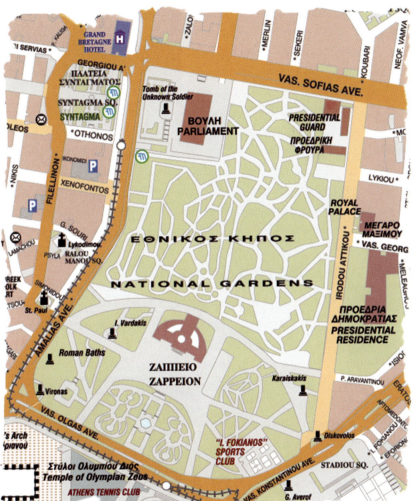

SYNTAGMA SQUARE

Syntagma Square (also known as Constitution Square) is bordered by Georgiou Avenue to the north, Othonos Street to the south, Filellinon Street to the west and Amalias Avenue to the east. The eastern side of the square is higher than the western and you need to go up a number of stairs in order to reach Amalias Street. Named after the Constitution of 1843, this marble-built square is the most famous in the country and has been center to both the political and social life of the Greeks. Lined with plenty of fast food restaurants, famous hotels, tourist agencies and tourist shops, Syntagma is always bustling with action. The city

renovation for the 2004 Olympics and the opening of a new metro station transformed this into a fabulous square. Walk around the marble pavement and huge water fountain, sit on one of the many benches or at one of the outdoor cafes and watch the action; something is always happening here. And afterwards, don't forget to check out the beautiful metro station; it is truly a museum that displays so many extraordinary finds from the excavations.

SYNTAGMA METRO STATION

Welcome to the Syntagma Square Metro station - one of the most magnificent stations in the world! Whether you chose to walk down the marble stairs or ride the multi-level escalators, you are suddenly immersed into an intermixed world of high tech and archaeology. Stunning modern sculptures among breathtaking pieces of antiquity are displayed throughout this mega-museum train station. When the new metro stations were being built, work was quite delayed

because every time the workers began to dig, a new archaeological find appeared. In the end, Greece had gained incredible new works of art dating from the Neolithic period to the present. Among the many discoveries, a bathhouse, metal working shops, aqueducts and cisterns, ancient roads, and city walls emerged from underground that have now found their home in the metro museums. Ancient grave stones, a 2,000 year old beehive, and a mosaic from the 5th century AD are among the fabulous treasures displayed in the Syntagma Square Metro Station. The other Metro stations also have some very fine exhibits. So as you are walking around town and pass one of these metro stations, be sure to pop in; you don't need to take a train or buy a ticket to visit!

Parliament Building - Old Palace

As you climb up the eastern stairs to Amalias Street, you will notice a large yellowish-golden building. This is the Parliament Building. This neoclassical building was the first building constructed in Syntagma Square by the German architect, Friedrich von Gartner. It was built in 1847 as the Old Palace for King Otho who resided there until 1862. It remained a palace until 1922 when Prime Minister Eleftherios Venizelos had it remodeled and turned it into the country's parliament building. The Monument of the Unknown Soldier was also added at this time.

Tomb of the Unknown Soldier

The Tomb of the Unknown Soldier stands in front of the Parliament. Built in 1929-30 and designed by the architect Emmanuel Lazardis, the monument is a cenotaph - a tomb or monument erected in honor of the fallen soldiers of war. On the wall around the tomb, you will notice many Greek letters. These are writings from Pericles' funeral oration, inspired by a sculpture on the pediment of the ancient Temple of Aphaia, located on the island of Aegina. In the middle of the wall there is a sculpture, created by the sculptor, Fokion Rok, which depicts a naked dead soldier with his armor. On both sides of the monument, there are copper plates listing all of the military events in which Greece has taken part since the Greek War of Independence (1821).

The Evzones

You may be wondering who those tall, handsome, fit men are that are standing in front of the canopy covered sentry boxes, guarding the Tomb of the Unknown Soldier. And why in the world are they dressed in kilted skirts? They are *Evzones*, or *Tsoliades*: the soldiers of the Presidential Guard dressed in the traditional 19th century costume from Southern Greece. The outfits are similar to those worn by the Klephts who fought in the 1821 War of Independence.

The Evzones' uniform is very elaborate. It takes 80 days to make each costume. There are a few different types of costumes that change according to the season. The summer outfit is a beige color (as you will notice in the photos), and in the winter it is blue-black. On special occasions, and on the grand changing of the guard on Sunday, the Evzones are dressed in the traditional white *foustanella* (skirt) that has 400 pleats (representing the 400 years of Turkish occupation) and a white shirt with wide sleeves. The costume is worn over white wool stockings with a black tassel tied around the knee. We can see that the Evzones are wearing red leather shoes adorned with pompoms; they are called *tsarouchia*. Each shoe has 60 nails studded in its sole and each pair weighs about 3 kilos. The Evzones also wear an embroidered waist coat, with a cartridge belt around the waist and a red garrison *fessi* (cap) that symbolizes the blood spilled in wars. A long black silk tassel hangs from this cap. On certain ceremonial occasions, you will also notice some Cretan costumes worn by the Presidential Guard. Each Evzone is responsible for ironing his own skirt and keeping his uniform in perfect condition.

It is a real honor, but very tedious work to be an Evzone. First of all, the guard must be at least six feet tall. In addition, he must be good looking, of sound character and have a lot of stamina. While on duty, the Evzones are not allowed to make facial expressions or talk to anyone; they must look straight ahead. Each guard is on duty for one hour, every six hours, meaning four times in a twenty-four hour watch.

The monument is guarded twenty-four hours and every hour there is a changing of the guard ritual - something that you must see. Three Evzones arrive, marching in from their camp behind the parliament. One Evzone actually brings two new Evzones and collects the other two that have been on duty. As you can see in the photos, the guards walk with the right arm up in the air. The left arm holds the gun. Their right foot is kicked against the ground from time to time and stretches forward to move ahead. The 11:00 AM Sunday changing of the guards is very elaborate with a marching band accompanied by the entire Presidential guard - try not to miss it.

Returning west through Syntagma Square, the first street is Filellinon Street, a street dedicated to foreigners who had loved

FOOTSTEPS THROUGH ATHINA

Greece and expressed their support for the country by taking an active role in its struggle for independence. In addition to several office buildings and shops that surround the area, the street has a number of interesting churches to see. The photo here is from the International Cow Parade, a temporary exhibition that originated in Chicago and came to Athens from May-August, 2006. Artists created 77 Greek-themed cows.

SOTIRA LYKODIMOU CHURCH RUSSIAN ORTHODOX

Odos: Filellinon Street

The Church of the Savior (Sotira) of Lykodimou is the parish church of the Russian community. It is the largest medieval building in Athens and one of the most important Byzantine monuments of the 11th century. During the Byzantine period and Ottoman rule, the church was a *katholikon* (main church) of a monastery. Throughout this time, Sotira Lykodimou suffered extensive damage from natural disasters (earthquakes) and wars, especially with the invasion of Francesco Morosini and the Greek War of Independence.

In 1847, the Russian Government purchased the church. In 1850, Tsar Alexander II restored it and added a heavy bell tower. Several post-Byzantine mural paintings were replaced by paintings of the German artist Ludwig Thiersch. In addition, the marble Byzantine screen was replaced by a tall, Russian version.

This church is recognizable by its enormous scale and its domed octagon which actually is quite low for its size. Its brickwork is composed of rich patterns with decorative elements embedded into the stone.

St. Paul Anglican-Episcopal Church
Odos: 29 Filellinon

The Anglican-Episcopal Church of St. Paul is located between Filellinon and Amalias Streets. It was founded and built in 1838 with funding from Athens' small Anglican community. Built in a Victorian, neoclassical setting, the walls and architrave of the church are made of marble from the Hymittos Mountain, while the main door and windows are made from Corinthian stone. The inscriptions on the windows, wall and furniture commemorate several Philhellenes who participated in the Greek War of Independence. This church is an important center for the English speaking community of Athens.

National Gardens

Walk a bit down Amalias Street and visit the beautiful National Gardens. The park used to be the garden of the Royal Palace. It was created by Queen Amalia and her German gardener, Schmidt. In the 1920's it opened to the public and now belongs to the Municipality of Athens.

It is one of the coolest and shadiest places to be on a hot summer day and it is a great place to escape and relax among many beautiful flowers, trees, birds and archaeological ruins. There are also many things for kids to see and do in this park. You can visit: two duck ponds, a children's playground, a small zoo, a Botanical Museum, and a children's library. And, if you get hungry, you can stop at the small café to eat some Greek appetizers, get a drink or perhaps some ice cream. On the southeast side of the park, you can view the busts of Kapodistrias, the first governor of Greece and of Eynard, a great Philhellene. On the south side, there are busts of two great poets: Kostas Solomos, who wrote the Greek national anthem and who was often seen strolling through this park; and that of Aristotelis Valaoritis, who is known for his patriotic poems.

There are four entrances that lead into the garden. The main entrance on Amalias; the central gate on Vasillis Sophias Avenue; one on Herodou Attikou Street; or from the gate that connects the National Gardens with Zappeion Park.

Zappeion Exhibition Hall

The Zappeion Hall is a beautiful classical style building adjacent to the National Gardens on the south side. It was built in 1888 in memory of Evangelos Zappas, a prosperous Greek businessman and philanthropist from Romania who was responsible for the revival of the modern Olympic Games. Through his contributions and dedication, he succeeded in reviving the Olympic Games in a city square in Athens: he also succeeded in refurbishing the Panathenian Stadium. In 1896, Zappeion Hall was the main building of the Olympic Village used for the first modern Olympic Games. Unfortunately, Zappas had died before this time and never witnessed the historical event. It was also here at

FOOTSTEPS THROUGH ATHINA

Zappeion Hall where the signing for Greece's accession to the European Economic Community took place on May 29, 1979.

You must stop in to see this magnificent building. Upon entering, walk over to the large oval area that is surrounded by a two-story colonnade adorned with caryatid-like columns. It is gorgeous! If you are fortunate to be here in the winter time, you might consider ice-skating on the frozen rink in front of the building. Ah, how awe-inspiring to do so among such magnificent Athenian sites!

ARCHAEOLOGICAL SITE OF ROMAN BATHS

As you walk south down Amalias Street, you will approach the Roman baths; a fairly new site of archaeological ruins that were discovered during the Athens Metro construction. Built in the late 3rd or 4th century AD, this site is in an excellently preserved state. It is covered by a metallic canopy. If you have the chance to be here at night, you will be impressed at how it stands out amongst the treasures in this area.

Footsteps Through Athina

SYNTAGMA SQUARE AND SURROUNDING AREA

 HELPFUL GREEK WORDS

Η Πλατεία Συντάγματος • Ee Plateea Seentagmatos • Syntagma (Constitution) Square

Ο Σταθμός Συντάγματος (Μετρό) • O Stathmos Seentagmatos (Metro) • Syntagma Metro Station

Η Βουλή • Ee Voulee • The Parliament

Το Μνημείο του Αγνώστου Στρατιώτη • To Mnemeeo tou Agnostou Strateeotee • The Tomb of the Unknown Soldier.

Οι Εύζωνες • Ee Evzones • The Evzones

Η Οδός Φιλελλήνων • Ee Odos Feeleleenon • Filellinon Street

Ο Ναός Αγίου Λυκοδήμου • O Naos Ayeeoo Leekodeemou • The Church of St. Lykodimou

Ο Ναός Αγίου Παύλου • O Naos Ayeeou Pavlou • St. Paul Church

Ο Εθνικός κήπος • O Ethneekos Keepos • The National Gardens

Το Ζάππειο Μέγαρο • To Zapeeo Megaro • Zappeion Hall

Τα Ρωμαϊκά Λουτρά • Ta Romayeeka Loutra • The Roman Baths

The Grande Bretagne Hotel, a landmark in Syntagma Square

64

FOOTSTEPS THROUGH THE OLYMPIC AREA

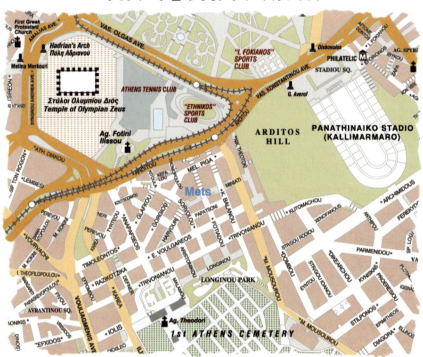

HADRIAN'S ARCH

Hadrian's Arch is next to the Temple of Zeus on Amalias Street. It divides the old city of Athens and the newer Roman section that was built by Emperor Hadrian. It was erected by the Athenians in 131 AD in honor of the emperor. Two inscriptions are carved on each side of the archetype. The one on the side facing the Acropolis reads: "This is Athens, the ancient city of Theseus," and the one on the other side that faces the new city reads: "This is the new city of Hadrian and not Theseus". The arch is made of Pentelic marble and crowned by a series of Corinthian columns and pilasters.

FOOTSTEPS THROUGH ATHINA

MELINA MERCOURI STATUE

Odos: Amalias St. & Dionysiou Aeropagitou St. (Across from Hadrian's Arch)

This statue honors Melina Mercouri, who played an enormous role in promoting Greek culture and in attempting to bring the Elgin Marbles back home to Greece. She is truly a role model and one of my favorite persons in Greek modern history.

TEMPLE OF OLYMPIAN ZEUS

The ruins of the Temple of Olympian Zeus are located East of Hadrian's Arch. The building of the temple began around 515 BC but was never finished until many centuries later, when in 125 AD the Roman Emperor Hadrian funded its completion. He dedicated the temple to Zeus Olympios during the Pan-Hellenic festival.

The Pentelic marble temple was originally surrounded by 104 Corinthian columns, but only fifteen remain today. There was a colossal ivory and gold statue of Zeus inside the temple and next to it stood a statue of the Emperor Hadrian. Unfortunately, they are no longer there; throughout the centuries, earthquakes and looting has destroyed the temple.

Footsteps Through Athina

Agia Fotini • Saint Fotini Church

Odos: Kallirois & Arditou Streets

Saint Fotini Samaritissa is located at the beginning of Kallirois Street, near the Olympeion. This is where the bank of the river Illisos used to be. It is a very popular church for ceremonies since it is surrounded by a park. It was built in 1872 and has been in renovation since 1986. According to legend, the church was built on an ancient monument dedicated to the goddess Hekate. During the 1830's the site was used as the Bavarian soldier's cemetery.

The Panathenaic Kallimarmaro Stadium

The Panathenaic or Kallimarmaro (Beautifully Marbled) Stadium is located in downtown Athens, east of the National Gardens and Zappeion Mansion. It was originally built for the Panathenaic Competitions during the ancient times. In 330 BC, Lykourgos rebuilt it in marble. It was then enlarged to a capacity of 50,000 and reopened by Herodes Atticus between the years of 140-144 AD. During the centuries, marble was stolen from the stadium and used for the construction of other buildings. In 1870 it was discovered in excavations, remodeled, and used for the very first modern Olympic Games in 1896.

The huge stadium is the only one in the world totally made out of white marble. In more recent years, the stadium has hosted special events, such as the 1997 Opening Ceremony of the World

Footsteps Through Athina

Athletics Championship. When the Greek national soccer team won the 2004 European Football Championship, a huge celebration took place here. At the 2004 Olympic Games, the Panathenaic Stadium hosted the archery competition and was also the finishing point for the men's and women's marathon races.

Philatelic Museum

Odos: 5 Stadiou Avenue & Fokianou (next to the Panathenaic Stadium)
Hours: Monday-Friday 8:00am-2:00pm

For all of you philatelists (stamp collectors), don't forget to check out this museum. Founded in 1978 and situated on a small street next to the Panathenaic Stadium, it boasts a fine collection of world stamps, but truly portrays the history of Greek stamps (beginning in 1861) as well as the development of the Greek post office. You can view the first Greek stamp ever (that of Hermes), and the Olympic stamp which is considered to be the rarest Greek stamp of all. In addition, you can glimpse at mail bags, safes, stamp machines and other items related to the Hellenic postal service. The museum also has a library with specialized books and magazines.

HELPFUL GREEK WORDS

Η Πύλη του Ανδριανού • Ee peelee tou Andrianou • Hadrian's Arch

Το άγαλμα της Μελίνας Μερκούρης • To Agalma tees Meleenas Merkourees • The Statue of Melina Mercouri

Ο Ναός Ολυμπίου Διός • O Naos Oleembeeou Deeos • Temple of Olympian Zeus

Η Αγία Φωτεινή • Ee Ayeea Foteenee • Saint Fotini

Το Παναθηναϊκό Στάδιο • To Panatheenayeeko Stadeeo • The Panathenaic Stadium

Το Καλλιμάρμαρο • To Kalleemarmaro • The Kallimarmaro

Το Φιλοτελικό Μουσείο • To Feeloteleeko Mouseeo • The Philatelic Museum

FOOTSTEPS AROUND THE NEIGHBORING AREAS

FIRST ATHENS CEMETERY

Odos: Anapafseos & Ilioupoleos Street

Immediately southwest of the Olympic Stadium, Anapafseos Street (Street of Repose) branches off from Arditou Street. It runs into the main Athenian cemetery, or First Athens Cemetery as it is called. It was founded in 1837 when Athens gained its independence from the Turks. Many famous Greek politicians, revolutionary war heroes, poets, artists and singers are buried here. Among those are: Melina Mercouri (actress & activist), Andreas Papandreou (Former Prime Minister of Greece), George Papandreou, Sr. (three time former Prime Minister of Greece), George Seferis (poet & Nobel Prize winner), Manos Hadjidakis (Greek composer), Heinrich Schliemann (archaeologist) and Aliki Vouyiouklaki (Greece's beloved actress).

When you first walk through the modern entrance hall, you will see a chapel on your left. The graves of the archbishops of Athens are located here. In contrast with other famous cemeteries around the world that are gloomy and Gothic looking, the Athens Cemetery is cozy and peaceful. Whitewashed tombstones adorned with photos of the deceased, beautiful statues inspired from the Romantic period, well-tended gardens filled with olive and pine trees and the smell of

Footsteps Through Athina

incense burning all add to the serenity of this cemetery. And the statues are a real work of art exemplifying the quality of marble carving attained in Greece between 1850 and 1920. Many of the sculptures were made by the finest sculptors from the island of Tinos. One of the most famous sculptures is the Sleeping Maiden, a classicist work by Giannoulis Chalepas (1878). The sculpture, on the tomb of Sofia Afentaki, displays a girl that appears to be asleep and not dead. This corresponds to the view of the Classicist period in which death is an eternal, dreamless sleep. This cemetery should definitely be on your list of places to visit. It is well worth seeing the beautiful sculptures and tombs of those Greeks who were so renowned throughout Greece's history.

The District of Mets

While you are walking around the area north of the cemetery, a good place to visit (especially if you are hungry) is the district of Mets. It is located between the Panathenaic Stadium and the First Athens Cemetery. The neighborhood was named Mets after a local restaurant on the Ilisso riverbank. Mets is well known for its great restaurants and clubs.

 HELPFUL GREEK WORDS

Το Πρώτο Νεκροταφείο Αθηνών • To <u>Proto</u> Nekrota<u>fee</u>o Athee<u>non</u> • Athens First Cemetery

Η Συνοικία Μετς • Ee Seenee<u>kee</u>a Mets • The District of Mets

FOOTSTEPS THROUGH ATHINA

FOOTSTEPS THROUGH PLAKA

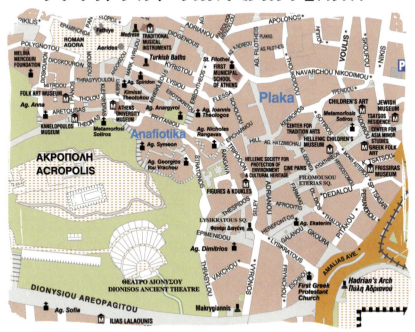

INTRODUCTION

Plaka, the oldest and most historical neighborhood of Athens, is located directly Northeast under the Acropolis. Its narrow, pedestrianized streets lined with 19th century neoclassical homes, Byzantine churches, and charming terraced restaurants and cafés make it a favorite spot among tourists and Athenians. You will feel as if you are traveling back in time while wandering through its museums, historical monuments, and ancient sites. In addition, it's great for souvenir shopping and the one place where you can bargain for the best price.

The exact origin of Plaka's name is still a bit unclear. Some people believe that

71

PLAKA

the name is derived from the Greek word, *plaka*, meaning a large stone slab which was found near the church of Agios Georgios that we will soon visit. The second possibility is that it originates from the Albanian word *pliaka*, meaning "old", a name that the sixteenth century Arvanites (Albanians) used to describe the area in which they lived.

Plaka is not very big; however, it is a bit of a labyrinth and has many small streets and alleys. It is easy to get lost, but not to worry; don't be afraid to ask for directions - everyone in this country loves to give advice! Once you familiarize yourself with the neighborhood, you can easily walk from one side to the other in less than twenty minutes. It also helps that cars are prohibited from entering most streets in this district.

Adrianou Street (running north and south) is the largest and most central street in Plaka and divides it into two areas: the upper level, - Ano Plaka - located right under the Acropolis and the lower level - Kato Plaka - situated between Syntagma and Monastiraki.

For your convenience, this chapter also divides Plaka into the two sections (Upper & Lower Plaka).

You can enter Plaka from various locations:
From the West Side of the Acropolis:
• Take Theorias Street that will lead you to the Upper Plaka (the Anafiotika district);
From the South Side of the Acropolis:
• Take Dionysiou Aeropagitou east and turn left at the first street, Thrassylou, that leads into Stratonos (this too will lead you to Anafiotika)
From Syntagma Square:
• Follow Ermou Street, or Mitropoleos Street, and turn left at any street leading south.

FOOTSTEPS THROUGH ATHINA

UPPER PLAKA · ANAFIOTIKA

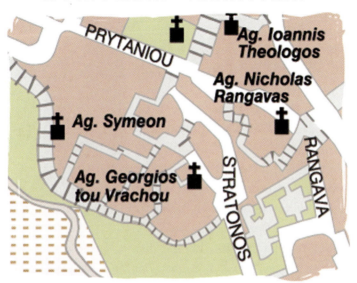

PLAKA

Anafiotika (little Anafi) is a small community on the northeastern slope of the Acropolis and is often referred to as Upper Plaka. Its boundaries stretch from Agios Georgios tou Vrachou Monastery (to the east) and Agios Symeon Monastery (to the west). It can be reached from Lower Plaka by climbing the stairs ascending towards the Acropolis.

The district of Anafiotika originates from the days of the Greek revolution when stonemasons (called Anafiotes) were brought from the Cycladic island of Anafi to build the king's palace and other main buildings. They settled in this area, and, in trying to overcome their homesickness, built their traditional island style houses on the steep slopes of the Acropolis. During this time, around three hundred residents lived in the area; unfortunately, today

73

FOOTSTEPS THROUGH ATHINA

PLAKA

very few people reside in the existing sixty houses. You seldom see anyone around but can often hear music and television coming from opened windows adorned with traditional, hand embroidered, lace-trimmed curtains.

Anafiotika is my favorite part of Athens. It is so fun walking through this island-like neighborhood of hidden, narrow, cobblestone paths and tiny, white-washed houses. Painted, clay pots filled with flowers and plants add a special touch to the balconies and rooftops of this quarter. It is very picturesque and a great place to take photos. There is also a fantastic panoramic view of the city from the top of this spot. And one thing for sure, you will be greeted by dozens of local cats that can be found everywhere. Again, do not forget your camera; your friends will truly think that you have been to an enchanting Greek island.

You can reach this area from the following locations:
• From the Parthenon, take Theorias Street; this will lead you directly into the top of the town.
• Coming from the Mitropoleos, take Mniskleous Street up to Theorias Street.

HELPFUL GREEK WORDS
Τα Αναφιώτικα • Τα Ana<u>feeo</u>teeka • Anafiotika

FOOTSTEPS THROUGH ATHINA

ST. GEORGE OF THE ROCK

Odos: Stratonos - on the Southeast Side of Anafiotika

St. George is a tiny, aisle-less, whitewashed, Cycladic island-type church that was built in the 17th century and then renovated by the Anaphiote craftsmen when they moved into the quarter after the Greek War of Independence. It was named St. George of the Rock because it is located at the

bottom of the Acropolis rock. The church is very charming and has a small courtyard filled with flowers. It also contains a memorial stone dedicated to Konstantinos Koukidis: a guard who wrapped himself in the Greek flag and then threw himself from the Acropolis to his death when the Germans marched into Athens in 1941.

ST. SYMEON

Odos: Theorias - western side of Anafiotika

The neoclassical church of St. Symeon was originally built in the 17th century, and reconstructed by the Anafiotes in 1847. It was built and decorated with red and yellow stripes to resemble the nearby Athens Cathedral, whose dome is visible from this point. A copy of the famous miracle-working icon of Panagia (the Virgin Mary) of Kalamiotissa can be found at this church. Celebrations are held here twice a year.

 HELPFUL GREEK WORDS

Ο Ναός του Αγίου Γεωργίου • O Na<u>os</u> tou A<u>gee</u>ou Yior<u>gee</u>ou • Church of Agios Georgios-St. George

Ο Ναός του Αγίου Συμεών • O Na<u>os</u> tou A<u>gee</u>ou Syme<u>on</u> • Church of St. Symeon

FOOTSTEPS THROUGH ATHINA

PLAKA

ANO • UPPER PLAKA • WESTERN SECTION

If you follow Theorias Street going west, you will approach another section of Upper Plaka lined with interesting museums and several beautiful churches. Let's take a peak at what this neighborhood has to show us.

ATHENS UNIVERSITY MUSEUM

Odos: Tholou 5
Hours: Monday – Friday: 9:30 am - 2:30 pm

One of the acts of the newly independent Greek state was to turn this private mansion into the first University of Athens. It was first used as a high school in 1835 for one year and, in 1837, was inaugurated as the Greek University of Otho (the king of Greece). In 1841 the university was relocated on Panepistimiou (Eleftheriou Venizelou) Street. The original building was then used as the Public Secretariat of Education and Ecclesiastical Affairs until 1850. During the Asia Minor Catastrophe of 1922, it housed several refugee families. Today, the museum is recognized as one of Greece's cultural heritage buildings. You can view rare books and manuscripts on subjects of law, medicine, theology and natural science and also scientific instruments, photos, and teaching aids that were used during the 19th century.

Church of the Metamorphosis
Odos: Theorias

This 14th century small Byzantine church operates today as a chapel for St. Nicholas of Ragavas Church, which we will shortly visit along our stroll through Plaka. The date of its construction is often questioned. Some people say that it was built in the 11th or early 12th century while others insist that it was built in the 14th. You will notice that the brick of this church is rough in some areas, indicating that it was built at different times. The base of the church is carved in marble and probably dates back to the Byzantine period. The tomb of Odysseas Androutsos, a war hero of the Greek War of Independence, can be found outside of the church. He was imprisoned on the Acropolis and his broken body was found on the Temple of Nike in June, 1825.

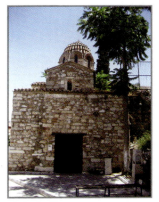

Kanellopoulos Museum
Odos: Theorias 12 (corner of Panos Street)
Hours: Tuesday - Sunday: 8:30 am - 2:00 pm

On the edge of Plaka, near the Metamorphosis Church, stands a beautiful mansion decorated with *acroteria* (sculptured roof ornaments) that was built in 1884. It was turned into the Kanellopoulos Museum in 1976 after Paul and Alexander

Kanellopoulos donated their private collection to the Greek state.

Upon your arrival, you can view Greek art from the 8th century BC up to the 19th century AD. The collection includes icons from the 14th to 17th centuries; selections of Byzantine, Persian and Mycenaean gold and jewelry; vases and jugs dating to the 8th century BC; Minoan, Phoenician, Egyptian, and Italian art; and a 2nd century marble head of Alexander the Great. Everything is well displayed throughout several floors of the mansion and you should have no problems reading about all these great treasures since all of the information is written in both Greek and English!

St. Anna Church

Odos: Dioskouron

After leaving the museum, walk to the corner of Theorias, turn right on Dioskouron, and you will see a tiny Cycladic style church to your right. This is St. (Agia) Anna Church and according to local records,

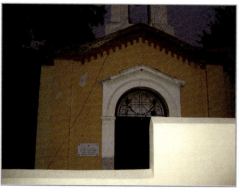

there was originally another church with the same name built on this site. The first church was built on top of the remains of an ancient temple dedicated to Artemis (goddess of child birth) and Apollo Pythios. Inside was a statue of Artemis. It is believed that St. Anna is the protector of pregnant women.

FOOTSTEPS THROUGH ATHINA

FOLK ART MUSEUM • MAN & TOOLS

Odos: Panos & Thoulou
Hours: Tuesday - Sunday:
9:00 am - 2:00 pm

This is a branch of the Museum of Greek Folk Art that specializes in its collections of tools to professions. It aims at familiarizing visitors with the concept of work in traditional societies.

KIMISSI THEOTOKOU/CHRISOKASTRIOTISSA OUR LADY OF THE GOLDEN CASTLE

Odos: Aliberti & Thrasyvoulou

The single nave church of Agia Maria Chrisokastriotissa was built in the 17th century. It is dedicated to the Assumption of the Virgin Mary of the *kastro* (castle/Acropolis). It is believed that during the Ottoman Occupation, this church always had an oil lamp burning in honor of the Virgin Mary that cured sick children. Additionally, it is believed that when the Ottoman forces entered the Acropolis in 1456, women and children sought refuge in the fortified castle (kastro) above. They had decided to jump from the walls to avoid capture, but the miraculous icon of the Virgin Mary saved them. The church still remains a refuge for women and children of today.

Footsteps Through Athina

Agios Spiridon & Agia Zoni tis Panagias
St. Spyridon & Sacred Belt of Virgin

Odos: Lysiou - just east of Markou Avriliou

In a populated area of Plaka stands the Church of the Sacred Belt of the Virgin & St. Spyridon, that was built during the 16th or 17th century. It is easy to miss this simple, light colored church, painted with reddish-brown trim that has never undergone restoration since it is tucked in between two restored houses.

 **HELPFUL GREEK WORDS**

΄Ανω Πλάκα-Δυτική Πλευρά • **A**no **Pla**ka Deetee**kee** Plev**ra** • Upper Plaka-Western Side

Το Μουσείο ιστορίας Πανεπιστημίου Αθηνών • **T**o Mou**see**o eesoto**ree**as Panepeestee**mee**ou Athee**non** • History Museum of the University of Athens

Ο Ναός της Μεταμορφώσεως του Σωτήρος • O Na**os** tees Metamor**fo**seos tou So**tee**ros • Metamorphosis Church of the Sotiros (Transfiguration of the Saviour-Sotirakis)

Το Μουσείο Κανελλοπούλου • To Mou**see**o Kanello**pou**lou • Kanellopoulos Museum

Η Αγία ΄Αννα • Ee A**gee**a **A**na • St. Anna

Το Μουσείο Εργαλείων • **T**o Mou**see**o Erga**lee**on • Museum - Man & Tools

Η Κοίμηση Θεοτόκου • Η Αγία Μαρία Χρυσοκαστριώτισσα • Ee **Kee**meesee Theo**to**kou – H A**gee**a Ma**ree**a Chreesokastree**o**teesa • Our Lady of the Golden Castle

Η Αγία Ζώνη της Παναγίας - Ο ΄Αγιος Σπυρίδων • Ee A**gee**a **Z**onee tees Pana**gee**as - O A**gee**os Spee**ree**don • Sacred Belt of Virgin & St. Spryridon

FOOTSTEPS THROUGH ATHINA

KATO · LOWER PLAKA · NORTH SIDE

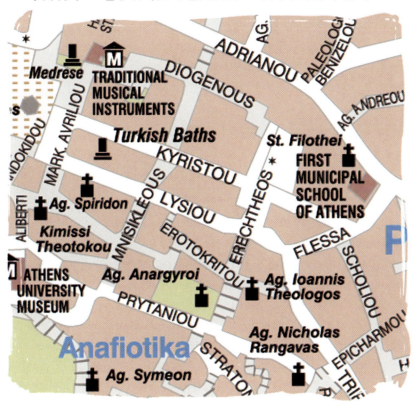

PLAKA

From St. Spyridon, make a right on Markou Avriliou. This will bring you to Kyristou street and the area of Lower Plaka.

BATHHOUSE OF THE WINDS · TURKISH BATHS

Odos: Kyrristou 8
Hours: All days except Tuesday:
9:00 am - 2:30 pm

The BathHouse of the Winds is the only public bath house that has survived in Athens today. Dating back from the period of the Turkish rule (1453-1669), it is near the Roman Forum and the Tower of the Winds. The baths functioned until 1965, and in 1984, the bath house was ceded to the Museum of Greek Folk Art. In 1989, restoration commenced, and in 1998, work was completed and the building became a museum. It is a fascinating place to visit! Once there, you can visit the three main rooms of the *hamams* (Turkish baths) which consist of the changing room, the *tepidarium* (warm bath room) and the *caldarium* (steam-sauna room).

Museum of Traditional Musical Instruments

Odos: Diogenous 3
Hours: Tues-Sun: 10:00 am - 2:00 pm
Wed: 12:00 pm - 6:00 pm

The Museum of Traditional Instruments is located in a neoclassical building. Upon your visit you can learn about all of the musical instruments that have been a part of Greek music since the 18th century. By viewing reproductions of frescoes, you can also acquaint yourself with Byzantine instruments, in addition to viewing the collections of drums, the gaida (Balkan windpipes), the santouri (sitar) and numerous other wind and percussion instruments originating from Asia, the Middle East, and Europe. The museum supplies headphones for you to listen to various types of Greek music. Don't forget to visit the gift shop where you can pick up some great CDs of traditional Greek music.

Plateia Paleas Agoras

Welcome aboard the Sunshine Express! If your feet are tired from walking, or you simply want to do something different, then you can take this small tourist train around the historical center of Athens and see the ancient sites and monuments in one single trip.

Footsteps Through Athina

Starting Point: Aiolou & Adrianou Streets-Plateia Paleas Agoras-Agora Square

Duration: 35 minutes

Hours of Departure: Every hour between 11:30 am to 2:30 pm & 5:00 pm to 12:00 am on weekdays from April 1 to September 30. Weekends - All year round: 11:00 am - 12:00 midnight

Train Passes by: Tower of the Winds; Adrian's Arch; Temple of Zeus; Herodes Atticus Theater; the Parthenon; the Propylaia; Pnyx Hill and Thission.

After leaving the Paleas Agoras Square, take Adrianou Street towards the Eastern side of Plaka; there is so much to see. Adrianou Street is Plaka's central thoroughfare and was the first street to be designed and paved in 1835. It is filled with tourist shops and some very old homes and buildings. Let's take a peek at a few of them!

House of St. Filothei

Odos: Adrianou 96

This is the house in which St. Filothei - a Greek Orthodox Saint, whose name was originally Rigoula Venizelou - resided during the Ottoman Occupation. She came from a very prominent family and studied to be a nurse. Shortly after she married, she was widowed and then became a nun helping Christian women who were taken to the Acropolis harem. This outraged the Ottoman authorities and eventually she was arrested, tortured, and died a martyr on February 19, 1589.

First Municipal School of Athens

Odos: Adrianou 106

This school was built in 1875 for the large sum of 40,000 drachmas. It was built over what was once a Turkish Mosque and before this, the archaeological site of Diogenes. The school is often referred to as the Kambanis School where Vassileios Kambanis taught from 1915-1938.

Church of Saints Anargyroi
Church of the Penniless

Odos: Erextheos 18

According to legend, the first church on this site was built in the 8th century by the empress Irene, an orphaned Athenian who later became the ruler of Byzantium after her husband died. The church was rebuilt in 1651 by Demetrios Kolynthis, a priest who came from a very wealthy family. At this time, a monastery was also added. During the Venetian siege of the Acropolis (1618-1694), the church was badly damaged and left abandoned until the 1700's when the Church of the Holy Sepulcher at Jerusalem acquired the property, which it still owns today.

This beautiful church was renovated in the 1800's. It has a gingerbread exterior and is surrounded by a small garden that contains fragments of ancient ruins. Its interior is done in the Baroque style and contains a carved and gilded iconostasis (icon screen).

St. Anargyroi is very famous among Athenians who come to receive the Holy Light that is flown in from Jerusalem and arrives

Footsteps Through Athina

first at this church for the midnight resurrection service. All over the country, it is tradition that Greek people await the Resurrection of Christ in dark, unlit churches. At midnight, the priests come out from the altar with the Holy Light (the flame represents the Resurrection) and pass it on to the faithful who are holding white, unlit candles. One by one, the candles are lit and the churches become illuminated by the Holy Light. This is a very popular church for weddings and baptisms.

Agios Ioannis Theologos
St. John the Theologian

Odos: Erechtheos & Erotokritou

Although there are no written records about the history of this tiny Byzantine church that is situated in a small square, we can assume that it was built in the 11th or 12th century. Its architecture - white stone and reddish bricks - is very characteristic of Byzantine monuments built during this period of time. It is one of the very few churches in Athens that is still intact with Byzantine murals.

Saint Nicholas Rangavas

Odos: Epicharmou & Tripodon

The church of Saint Nicholas Rangavas is the largest remaining Byzantine Church in Athens and is situated above the stairs of Prytaniou, a street named after the ancient city where a sacred flame used to burn. It was built in the 11th century by St. Pavlos of Xiropotamou, the grandson of the Emperor Michael I Rangavas. Some say that St. Nicholas was built on the site of an earlier church and that there may have been an ancient temple here as well. The church was constructed with bricks from ancient buildings and choragic monuments. In addition, the bricks outlining the windows exemplify the typical Byzantine style. The church was rebuilt in the early 20th century when the chapel of Agia Paraskevi was added and then restored in the late 1970's.

St. Nicholas is also a very historical site. In the 1821 Greek War of Independence, this was the first church to acquire church bells; something that had been banned during the Ottoman rule. It was also the first church to ring the bell signaling liberation from German Occupation on October 12, 1944. This church also remains a very popular church for both weddings and baptisms.

HELPFUL GREEK WORDS

Το Λουτρό των Αέρηδων • To Lou<u>tro</u> ton <u>Ae</u>reedon • The Bathhouse of the Winds

Το Μουσείο Λαϊκών Οργάνων • To Moo<u>see</u>o Lae<u>kon</u> Or<u>ga</u>non • Museum of Traditional Musical Instruments

Η Πλατεία Παλαιάς Αγοράς • Ee Pla<u>tee</u>a Pal<u>eas</u> A<u>goras</u> • Paleas Agoras Square

Η Αγία Φιλοθέη • Ee A<u>gee</u>a Feelo<u>thay</u>ee • St. Filothei

Το Πρώτο Δημοτικό Σχολείο • To <u>pro</u>to demoti<u>ko</u> scho<u>leeo</u> • The 1st Municipal School

Οι ΄Αγιοι Ανάργυροι Κολοκύνθοι • Ee A<u>gee</u> A<u>nary</u>eeree Kolo<u>keen</u>thee • Saints Anargyroi Kolynthi

Ο ΄Αγιος Ιωάννης ο Θεολόγος • O A<u>gee</u>os Eeo<u>a</u>nees o Theo<u>lo</u>gos • St. John the Theologian

Ο ΄Αγιος Νικόλαος Ραγκαβάς • O A<u>gee</u>os Nee<u>ko</u>leos Rangka<u>vas</u> • St. Nicholas Rangavas

FOOTSTEPS THROUGH ATHINA

KATO · LOWER PLAKA · EAST SIDE

PLAKA

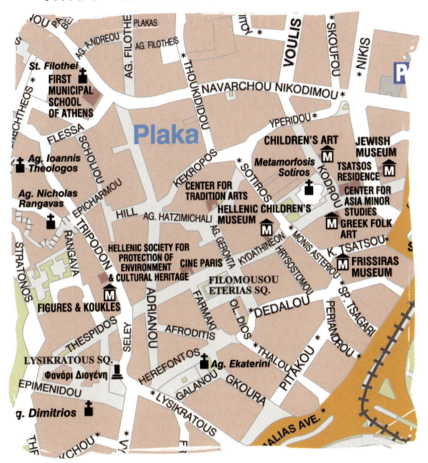

Make your way southeast to Tripodon Street, an antique street that used to be lined with bronze tripods awarded to the winning sponsors of competitions in music and drama. Today, this picturesque street is now lined with neoclassical homes, statues and unique shops, and is very enchanting to walk through.

87

FOOTSTEPS THROUGH ATHINA

HELLENIC SOCIETY FOR PROTECTION OF ENVIRONMENT & CULTURAL HERITAGE

Odos: Tripodon 28
Hours: Weekdays: 11:00 am – 6:00 pm

Since 1972, this center has been active in protecting the environmental and cultural heritage of Greece. In addition to several international and local programs, the Hellenic Society also develops an array of educational information and activities for environmental education in Greek Schools. Located in a beautiful, neoclassical house made of light rose stucco with grey and white trim, the center recently won an award for restoration. The center has a gift shop that sells environmental and cultural gifts, games and books and a clubhouse on the ground floor where you can eat lunch.

FIGURES & KOUKLES • PUPPET THEATER

Odos: Tripodon 30   **Hours:** Saturdays at 5:00 pm

If you would like to see how Greek children (and adults, too!) were entertained long before the days of technology, Figures and Koukles is definitely the place to visit. Here you can enjoy the Puppet Shadow Theater, or as we say in Greek, *Karaghiozis* (meaning black eyes in Turkish), and watch the handmade puppets as they appear before an illuminated white screen. This form of entertainment originated from eastern oriental countries and was very popular in Greece until the 1960's and 1970's. Unfortunately, not many puppet shows still exist in Greece today. Although the names of the puppets are Turkish, the characters are Greek and the performances represent the Greek struggle during the Turkish domination and War of Independence.

FOOTSTEPS THROUGH ATHINA

THE CHORAGIC MONUMENT OF LYSIKRATES

As you continue walking along Tripodon Street you will eventually reach Lysikrates Square. Here you can see the Choragic (chorus leader) Monument of Lysikrates. During classical times, it was customary for the sponsor of the winning theatrical troupe at the annual Dionysia theater competition to erect a marble stele (column) at a prominent spot. In 335 BC, Lysikrates (the sponsor of that year's winners) built the marble monument that included a dedication plaque. It is the last of the many monuments dedicated to the Dionysia competition on Tripodon Street.

The very well preserved monument is cylindrical in shape. It is based on a square foundation and has 6 Corinthian columns. It is the first monument of that time to use Corinthian columns whereas all the other monuments have incorporated the Doric or Ionic style.

Throughout the centuries, the Monument of Lysikrates went through many transformations. In 1669, it became part of a Cappuccin monastery and was renamed the Lantern of Diogenes. The monks used it as a reading room and a library. The monastery was destroyed during the Greek war of independence of 1821 and then restored in 1845 by a French archaeological team.

AGIOS DIMITRIOS CHURCH

Odos: Epimenidou

The church of St. Dimitrios is near the Monument of Lysikrates on Epimenidou St. This single-nave barrel vault church was built in the 17th century. It is a very famous church because this is where Athanasios Diakos, a leading figure in the Greek War of Independence, served as a deacon.

89

Herefontos-Agia Ekaterini St. Catherine Church

Odos: Herefontos & Lysikratous

Across from Lysikrates Square on Lysikratous St. you will see a big *periptero* (kiosk) and then behind it St. Catherine's Church or Herefontos (as it is known in Greek). It was built in the 11th century and originally named Agios Theodoros, but in 1767 it became a dependent monastery of Sina and from this point on was called St. Catherine. The church was built on an ancient site. The courtyard displays a Roman colonnade, and the main body of the church is Byzantine. Two chapels were added to this edifice in the first half of the 20th century. Today, the church features one of the best choirs in Athens.

Filomousou Eterias Square

Odos: Where Kydathineon, Farmaki & Geronta Streets meet

After leaving Agia Ekaterini, proceed on Herfontos Street, until you reach Adrianou Street. At this intersection, turn left on the historic street of Kydathinaion. Here you will find Filomousou Eterias Square (meaning "friends of the muses"), also known as *Plateia* (Square) Plakas. Founded in 1813, its objective was to promote Greek-oriented studies and to preserve the archaeological treasures of Athens. It's a lively area filled with several museums, cafes and outdoor tavernas, souvenir and jewelry shops, churches and a Jewish Synagogue. Let me point out a few great places worth visiting...

FOOTSTEPS THROUGH ATHINA

CENTER FOR TRADITION ARTS

Odos: Angelikis Chatzimichali 6 (at corner of Ang. Geronta)
Hours: Tuesday - Friday: 9:00 am - 1:00 pm & 5:00 pm - 9:00 pm

Here's another great place where you can learn all about the beautiful folk art and traditions of Greece. This center houses a fine collection of Greek costumes, embroidery, lace and weaving, in addition to musical instruments, ceramics, icons and religious artifacts.

In addition to the excellent collection, you must also pay close attention to this beautiful building that was originally the house of Angeliki Hatzimihali (considered the mother of Greek folklore) and designed in the 1920's. It certainly is an attraction with its high ceiling rooms and finely carved wooden doors, windows and stairs. The center contains a library and also offers classes pertaining to the many artifacts on display.

CINE PARIS

Odos: Kidathineon 22

You can't come to Greece without visiting an outdoor cinema. Outdoor theaters in Greece offer so much that you can't find back home. Here you can sit at a table, order food and drinks in an elegant environment and truly relax. It is so enjoyable during a hot summer evening to sit outside and watch a movie on a terrace beneath the Greek moonlit sky. And being that the Cine Paris Theater is under the Acropolis, the view is breathtaking, especially if you sit on the balcony. Oh, and not to worry; most of the movies are in English with Greek subtitles.

Footsteps Through Athina

PLAKA

Hellenic Children's Museum

Odos: Kydathineon 14
Hours: Tuesday - Friday: 10:00 am - 2:00 pm
Saturday & Sunday: 10:00 am – 3:00 pm

Here's another great place for children between the ages of 4 and 12 to gain direct hands-on experiences from museum artifacts and objects. Situated in an early 20th century neoclassical building, the two-floor museum offers an array of activities for children and also provides numerous seminar programs for adults. You will love the "grandmother and grandfather" room that depicts an old Athenian house filled with old furniture and objects. You can even dress up in costumes from the past. Make sure that you check out the museum's library and playground.

Frissiras Museum

Odos: Monis Asteriou 3 & 7 (street running off of Kidathineon)
Hours: Wed-Fri: 11:00 am - 7:00 pm
Sat-Sun: 10:00 am - 2:00 pm

In this beautifully restored, neoclassical gold and white terra-cotta building, you can view contemporary art of Greek and foreign artists.

This private museum was opened in December 2000 to house the collection of Vlassis Frissaris. It contains 3,000 visual art works (2,000 paintings and 1,000 drawings) by European and Greek painters from the 20th century.

FOOTSTEPS THROUGH ATHINA

PLAKA

KONSTANTINOS TSATSOS RESIDENCE
Odos: Kydathineon 9

At this site you can see the house of Konstantinos Tsatsos who was a scholar, professor of law and a politician. He served as the President of Greece from 1975-1980.

CENTER OF ASIA MINOR STUDIES
Odos: Kydathineon 11
Hours: Monday - Friday: 10:00 am - 2:00 pm

This building houses one of the most important ethnological research centers in Greece and highlights the musical and folk traditions of refugees from Asia Minor.

MUSEUM OF GREEK FOLK ART
Odos: Kydathineon 17
Hours: Tues - Sun: 10:00 am - 2:00 pm

Greek folk art is such an intricate part of Greek culture, and the country of Greece is

so rich in its collections. This museum is a favorite among children as it offers so much! It will give you an insight to the traditions and origins of Greek textile, silver works, ceramics, embroidery, lace and weaving such as those that you see displayed in the tourist shops around Plaka. View the beautiful collections of heirlooms, such as bed covers decorated with symbolic, narrative motifs and bed trimmings dating back from as early as the Ottoman

Occupation; along with the many ceramics, carnival costumes and also *Karaghiozi* characters. Be sure to check out the early 20th century murals of Theophilos Hadtzimihali (he is one of my favorites) in a side room of the museum. His scenes depict Greek peasant life or battle scenes during the War of Independence.

Agia Sotira Metamorfosis Sotira tou Kottaki

Odos: Kydathineon/Sotiros

The Church of the Metamorfosis (Transfiguration of the Saviour) or Kottakis (named after a prominent Athenian family) is one of the earliest Byzantine churches in Athens. It was originally built in the 12th century on the site of an older, 6th century building. We can verify this by viewing both the Apse on the eastern side of the church, and the cross shaped arrangement of the roof – remnants of the original church. During the Greek War of Independence, Agia Sotira suffered extensive damage. Shortly after, it served as a Russian Church. It underwent significant repairs in the early 20th century, including the addition of a bell tower. The courtyard has a bust of Konstantinos and Ioannou Tsatsos, the late president and wife of the Greek Republic.

Greek Children's Art Museum

Odos: Kodrou 9 (extension of Voulis Street)
Hours: Tuesday - Saturday: 10:00 am - 2:00pm
Sunday: 11:00 am – 2:00 pm

Since 1994, the Greek Children's Art Museum has offered the opportunity for children of all ages to learn through a fun, interactive experience. At this museum, you can view paintings and three dimensional artworks by Greek children up to 14 years old.

You can also explore the collection of children's toys from Africa and artwork from the Kalesh children of Pakistan. Several schools partake in fine educational programs the museum offers that aim in providing both a pleasant and creative experience for all children.

JEWISH MUSEUM OF GREECE

Odos: Nikis Street 39
Hours: Mon - Fri: 9.00 am - 2.30 pm
Sundays: 10:00 am – 2:00 pm
Saturdays: Closed

For more than two thousand years, Greece has been home to a number of thriving Jewish communities. From the end of 19th century and until the early 20th, Thessaloniki's Jewish community comprised more than half of the city's population. Unfortunately, during the Holocaust, 87% of the Jews in Greece perished and only about 5,000 remain today.

In this neoclassical building on Nikis Street, the Jewish Museum depicts the story of the Jews in Greece from the 3rd century BC to the Holocaust. The museum pays tributes to the two main Jewish communities throughout the country: the Romaniotes – whose presence dates back to the 3rd century BC, and the Ladino-speaking Sephardic Jews who were exiled from Spain during the Inquisition in 1492. The museum displays over 8,000 original artifacts that that bear witness to more than 23 centuries of the Jewish presence in Greece. One room displays a reconstruction of the interior of the old Romaniote Synagogue of Patras, a community established by Jews from Syria from 323-281 BC.

FOOTSTEPS THROUGH ATHINA

HELPFUL GREEK WORDS

Η Ελληνική Εταιρεία Για Την Προστασία Του Περιβάλλοντας και Της Π
ολιτιστικής Κληρονομίας • Ee Elleeneekee Etereea ya tin Prostaseea
tou Perivallontas kai tees Politistikees Kleeronomeeas • Hellenic
Society for Protection of Environment & Cultural Heritage

Φιγούρες και Κούκλες • Feegoures ke koukles • Figures & Koukles

Το Μνημείο του Λυσικράτους • To Mneemeeio tou Leeseekratous •
The Monument of Lysikrates

Ο ´Αγιος Δημήτριος • O Ageeos Deemeetreeos • St. Dimitrios

Η Αγία Αικατερίνη Χαιρεφώντος • Ee Ageea Ekatereenee
Herefontos • St. Catherine Herefontos

Η Πλατεία Φιλομούσου Εταιρίας • Ee Plateea Feelomousou
Etayreeas • Filomousou Eterias Square

Το Κέντρο Λαϊκής Τέχνης και Παράδοσης • To Kentro Laeekees
Teknees ke Paradosees • Center of Folk Arts & Traditions

Το θερινό σίνεμα • To thereeno seenema • The Outdoor Theater

Το Ελληνικό Παιδικό Μουσείο • To Elleeneeneeko Pedeeko Mouseeo
• Hellenic Children's Museum

Το μουσείο Φρυσίρα • To mouseeo Freeseera • The Firssiras
Museum

Ο Κωνσταντίνος Τσάτσος • O Konstanteenos Tsatstos • Konstantinos
Tsatsos

Το Κέντρο Μικρασιατικών Σπουδών • To Kentro Meekraseeatikon
Spoudon • Center of Asia Minor Studies

Το Μουσείο Ελληνικής Λαϊκής Τέχνης • To Mouseeo Eleeneekees
Laeekees Teknees • Museum of Greek Folk Art

Ο Ναός του Σωτήρος Μεταμορφόρσεως • O Naos tou Soteeros
Metamorfoseos • Church of the Metamorphosis

Η Αγία Σωτήρα Κοττάκη • Ee Ageea Soteera Kottakee • St. Sotira
Kottaki

Το Μουσείο Ελληνικής Παιδικής Τέχνης • To Mouseeo Eleeneekees
Teknees • Museum of Greek Children's Art

Το Εβραϊκό Μουσείο Ελλάδος • To Evrayeeko Mouseeo Ellados • The
Jewish Museum of Greece

FOOTSTEPS THROUGH MONASTIRAKI AND SURROUNDING AREA

You can't come to Athens without visiting Monastiraki Square and its surrounding areas. There are a number of ways to reach it. One way is by going through Plaka. If you happen to be in Syntagma Square, you can walk down Ermou or Mitropoleos Street. Let's take a quick look at both of these streets since there are a number of shops, churches and attractions that I would like to point out to you.

MITROPOLEOS & ERMOU STREETS

AGIA DINAMI • HOLY POWER OF THE VIRGIN

Odos: Mitropoleos St.

Agia Dinami is a tiny, small, barrel-vaulted church dedicated to the birth of the Virgin Mary. It is known as the church that protects women in labor; and up to this day, pregnant women come here to pray for a safe and painless delivery. Agia Dinami was built during the early years of Byzantine Rule and it is believed that before its construction there was a temple dedicated to Herakles on this site. The church is wedged between three pillars under a building that for years served as the Ministry of Education. Since it is a very historical church, it could not be demolished during construction and thus the building had to be built around the church. During the Greek War of Independence, the Greek ammunition master, Mastopavlis, was responsible for making bullets for the Turks in this church. However, he managed to make them for the Greek freedom fighters, too, and snuck them out in garbage bags during the night. When you visit Agia Dinami, you will notice a wall with painted icons of Agia Filothei, one of Athens' patron saints.

MITROPOLEOS SQUARE

We have arrived in Plateia Mitropoleos (Metropolitan Square), an exquisite and spacious marble paved square embraced by the Cathedral of Athens, outdoor cafés, tavernas and tourist stores. There are also some great souvlaki (meat in pita bread) shops around here; you can't leave Greece without trying some. The taste is  unbelievable! As we say in Greek: *Pame ekei* "Let's go over there!"

EVANGELISMOS THEOTOKOU · MITROPOLIS METROPOLITAN CATHEDRAL OF ATHENS

The Mitropolis Cathedral of Athens is dedicated to the Annunciation of the Virgin. It is a big, three-aisled, domed basilica that serves as the seat of the Bishop of Athens (who is also the Archbishop of Greece). Construction on this church began in 1842 and was completed twenty years later. The cost was tremendous and if it weren't for donations from King Otho, the wealthy Sinas family from Austria and other generous donors, it would have taken many more years to complete. It was built in four stages and work was often delayed due to financial problems. Among those that helped design and build it were: Theophilus Hansen, Francois Boulanger, Dimitris Zezos and

Panagiotis Kalkos. The church was built with material from 72 dilapidated Byzantine churches that were mainly ruined during the Greek War of Independence. Its interior is made up of different types of marble and contains numerous icons. There are also tombs of two martyrs from the Ottoman period: St. Filothei (read more about her in the Lower Plaka Section), whose bones are in a silver reliquary, and St. Gregory V (Patriarch of Constantinople), who was hung by the Turks and then thrown into the Bosporus Strait during the War of Independence. Greek sailors found his body and took it to Odessa. In 1871, the Pontian Greeks brought his bones back to Greece. You can see his statue in the square.

This Mitropolis Cathedral is considered to be the most important church in Athens and it is here where weddings and funerals of many famous Athenians take place. On Sundays and special feast days, the liturgy (Church service) is always televised from this church.

Panagia Gorgoepikoos
Agios Eleftherios • Little Mitropolis

Next to the Mitropolis stands a small Byzantine church dedicated to Panagia Gorgoepikoos (All saint Mary who answers quickly to prayers) and Agios Eleftherios. After King Otho was expelled, the church received its second name, *eleftherios*, which means "freedom" in Greek. It is also referred to as the Mikri Mitropoli, or Little Cathedral.

Panagia Gorgoepikoos was built at the end of the 12th century. It is believed that the church was founded by the Byzantine empress Irini around 787. During Ottoman rule, the church belonged to the Episcopal mansion and was called "katholikon". After Greece became a free country, it was used as the National Library.

The church is built as a cross-in-square with two inner columns that support the dome. It is made mostly of marble (bits taken from the Agora) and has very few bricks. The plaques on the outside wall are of particular importance dating back to the Classical and Byzantine Periods. They represent different historical periods and incorporate different types of design. Those from the 9th and 10th century consist of oriental designs (animals, plants), whereas the Byzantines ones depict oriental sphinxes, geometric shapes and animals. There are also trophies of the Panathenaic Games dating back to Ancient Greece. In an effort to Christianize these ancient sculptures, the artisans added a cross to the different scenes.

Ermou Street is named after Hermes, the god of commerce. What an appropriate name for the street that is considered to be the number one shopping paradise of downtown Athens! So if you are in the mood to shop, you have come to the right place. And great news - vehicles are prohibited on this street so you don't have to worry about being hit by speeding mopeds and cars as you are clinging to all your shopping bags. But beware: there are tons of shoppers out there, especially on Saturdays. As you are dashing from store to store, do take some time to enjoy the sidewalk entertainment from mimes dressed in silver metallic costumes to bands, playing international tunes, and my favorite, the famous Laterna organ grinder, who plays nostalgic Greek music from the past. Welcome to Ermou Street; it's a great place for shopping therapy!

Among the many international designer name shops you can find: Zara, Mango, Esprit, LaCoste, Marks & Spencer Department Store, Benetton, Folli Follie (a fabulous Greek jewelry store); Replay, Nike and many more - including great shoe stores. For cosmetics and skin creams try Sephora, Body Shop and Hondos Center.

PANAGIA ROMVI • VIRGIN MARY OF ROMVI
Odos: Evangelistrias Street near corner of Ermou

Although there are no existing written documents of this church, the name Romvis, or Roumbis, refers to the church's founder. The name appears on official documents from the Ottoman period, verifying that there indeed was an Athenian family with this name. Panagia Romvi is a three-aisled basilica that most likely was built during the Ottoman era. Having suffered extensive damage, the church was eventually repaired and the external walls were altered. The aisles are covered by vaults with the central one ending in conches. On the northern side of the church, an additional building was added with two compartments, one serving as a chapel.

PANAGIA KAPNIKAREA (ST. MARY)
Odos: Ermou

As you are walking down Ermou Street towards Monastiraki, you will approach a church in the middle of the street. It is called Panagia Kapnikarea (St. Mary) and considered to be one of the most important Byzantine churches in Athens. Built in the mid 11th century, it is a tetra style, cross-in-square church with Kufic (imitation of Arabic scripts) brick patterns. A chapel dedicated to Saint Barbara was added to the northern side shortly after it was built. Throughout the centuries, many other additions were made. Several fine icons were added to its interior as well as exterior. During the War of Independence Ermou Street was severely damaged. Shortly after, the city had decided to tear down the church. However, King Otto's father, Ludwig of Bavaria, prevented this from happening. The church now belongs to the University of Athens.

Agia Irini • Saint Irene
Odos: Corner of Aiolou & Agias Eirinis Streets

This church was designed by Lysandros Kaftantzoglou in 1846. It was built on the site where another church dedicated to the same saint once stood. The old church was badly damaged during the Greek War of Independence. At first, the site was designated for the building of the city's Cathedral; however, when plans changed, the local community requested that the church of Saint Irene be rebuilt on this site. The neoclassical church was consecrated in 1850. It is a three-aisled domed basilica with three vaults, lobed windows on pediments and two bell towers at the end of the church.

 HELPFUL GREEK WORDS

Η Αγία Δύναμη • Ee A<u>yee</u>a <u>Dee</u>namee • Agia Dinami • Holy Power of the Virgin

Η Πλατεία Μητροπόλεως • Ee Pl<u>atee</u>a Meetr<u>opol</u>eos • Mitropoleos Square

Η Μητρόπολη-Ο Καθεδρικός Ναός της Αθήνας • Ee Me<u>etr</u>opolee-O Kathedree<u>kos</u> Na<u>os</u> tees A<u>thee</u>nas • The Metropolitan Cathedral of Athens

Η Παναγία Γοργοεπήκοος- Ο Άγιος Ελεύθερος • Ee Pana<u>yee</u>a Gorgoe<u>peek</u>oos- O A<u>yee</u>os El<u>eft</u>heros • All Saint Panagia-Mary-Saint Eleftheros

Η οδός Ερμού • Ee O<u>dos</u> Er<u>mou</u> • Ermou Street

Η Παναγία Ρόμβη • Ee Pana<u>yee</u>a Ro<u>mvi</u> • Panagia Romvi

Η Παναγία Καπνικαρέα •Ee Pana<u>yee</u>a Kapneeka<u>rea</u> • St. Mary

Η Αγία Ειρήνη • Ee A<u>yee</u>a Ee<u>ree</u>nee • St. Irini

FOOTSTEPS THROUGH ATHINA

MONASTIRAKI

Now let's head back to Ermou Street. Go west and take it directly to Monastiraki Square.

MONASTIRAKI SQUARE

Monastiraki (meaning "little monastery", since there once stood a monastery on this site from the 11th-16th century) is a very old historical section of Athens with remnants still standing among present-day modernity. It is a noisy, bustling hub where east meets west, filled with street vendors selling anything from lighters to jewelry, and waiters dashing across streets balancing trays of souvlaki or Greek coffee for patrons. The tiny streets around Monastiraki also have character, which we will soon visit. Be sure to check out the fabulous graffiti on one of the building's walls. It was designed by Alexandros Vasmoulakis, a graffiti artist who was commissioned to decorate various cityscapes for the Athens 2004 Olympics. For several decades, Monasti-

103

raki had lost its beauty and became a rather gloomy site. The square is currently undergoing construction, and its new facelift will restore its image, both historically and archaeologically.

Flea Market • Yusurum

Monastiraki is known for its flea market, *to Pazari*, and it's a bit confusing because there are actually two markets to visit. The first one is often referred to as Yusurum, a name derived from a Jewish antiques trader. This market starts at Monastiraki Square and continues down the street to Agios Phillippos and Abyssinia Square. You can find a number of small shops that are open daily and sell both old and new clothes and numerous old objects such as coins, medals, plates, old books, records and jewelry.

The other market is the big flea market that has been in existence since 1910 and takes place every Sunday here. You need to arrive early because it becomes very crowded around 11:00am. There are so many things for sale, from Greek antiques to modern day gadgets and furniture. It is really a lot of fun spending your Sunday morning here! And even better, the act of bargaining is very acceptable and truly the norm.

Panagia Pantanassa • Virgin Mary Queen of All

Odos: Monastiraki Square

While you are walking around Monastiraki, you will notice a rather small church. It is called Panagia Pantanassa (the Virgin Mary Queen of All). It used to be known as the Great Monastery and this is how the square took its name. The original monastery probably dated back to the 11th century and stretched from Athinas to Aiolou Streets. When the first metro was developed in 1896, the monastery buildings were demolished. It was a very important church up to this time, but lost its importance after the construction. The three-aisled, barrel-vaulted church that exists today was built in the 17th century. It formally belonged to the Monastery of Kaissariani on Hymittos Mountain and first served as a women's monastery. Later it became the Great Monastery and was known for its textile production. During the early 20th century, the church underwent repairs and also received a tall bell tower. Even today, conservation and repair work continue on this tiny, historical church.

MONASTIRAKI METRO

While in Monastiraki, you really must take a look at another archaeological gem, the Metro Station. This station is unique, for it is here that you can actually view the bed  of the Eridanos River, dating back to antiquity. The Eridanos River began at Lycavittos Hill, then through the Ancient Agora to the site of Keramikos where it is still visible today. Since Roman days - 200 AD - it had been covered with a clay roof and used as a sewer. Rediscovered during the start of excavations in 1992, this amazing exhibit displays the remains of three different periods of time, two of which are Roman and one of the Paleochristianic. The archaeological site is covered with a specially designed glass casing and has an attached pedestrian corridor that you can walk on top of to get a closer view.

Monastiraki is the last station of the Attiko Blue Line (Line 3) and serves as a changing point to Line 1 (Kifissia-Piraeus). (See the Practical Information section for more details of the Metro System.)

Tsisdarakis Mosque • Museum of Ceramics

Another interesting site in Monastiraki Square is the Tsisdarakis Mosque. Very few mosques have remained from the four centuries that Greece was under Turkish rule. After liberation, the Greeks wanted to erase all traces of this difficult period, so they destroyed the majority of buildings from this era. You can, however, find this mosque in the heart of Monastiraki. It was built in 1759 by Mustafa Aga Tsisdarakis. At one time there was a minaret next to it, but this too was destroyed after Greece was freed from the Turks. After Greek independence, the building was used for different purposes and has functioned as a guardhouse, a prison, a military camp and a warehouse.

In 1915, it was restored by Anastasios Orlandos. Three years later it became the Museum of Greek Handicrafts and in 1923 renamed the National Museum of Decorative Arts. In 1959, it became the Museum of Greek Folk Art. In 1973, the museum was transferred to another location and the mosque was used as an auxiliary building that housed collections of Greek ceramics. Ten years later it reopened again as the Museum of Ceramics. Be sure to stop by; you will get an idea of what the inside of a mosque is like and you will also see a fine collection of folk ceramics and pottery.

HELPFUL GREEK WORDS

Το Μοναστηράκι • To Monasterakee • Monastiraki

Το παζάρι • To Pazaree • To Pazari-Flea Market

Η Παναγία Παντάνασσα • Ee Panayeea Pantanassa • Panagia Pantanassa

Ο σταθμός Μοναστηράκι Μετρό • O Stathmos Monasteerakee Metro • Monastiraki Metro Station

Το Τζαμί Τζισταράκι • To Jamee Jeestarakee • The Tsisdarakis Mosque

FOOTSTEPS THROUGH ATHINA

THE ROMAN AGORA · FORUM

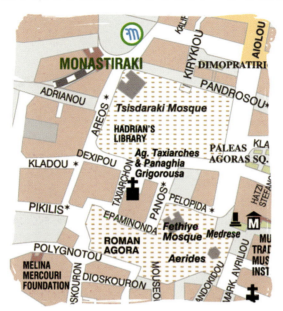

HADRIAN'S LIBRARY

Next to the mosque you will see the ruins of Hadrian's Library, which was built by the Roman emperor Hadrian in 132 AD. The entrance was on the west side and decorated with beautiful Corinthian columns. Even though it was called the library, it also served as a public square and a cultural center. The complex had a courtyard with a central pool and garden.

TETRACONCH MEGALI PANAGIA CHURCH

While you are at Hadrian's Library, you can see the remains of what is believed to be the oldest Christian Church in Athens, the Tetraconch. Situated in the courtyard of Hadrian's Library, the Tetraconch is a marble, central plan church that was founded in the 5th century AD. It consisted of a central square room with four conches (this is why it is called Tetraconch), interior colonnades, an interior corridor that surrounded the main room, a large narthex and atrium on the western side. You can still see parts of the foundations and the lower walls, as well as the remains of the mosaic floor.

The church was destroyed at the end of the 6th century, and in the 7th century a three nave basilica was constructed on this site. In the 12th century, Megali Panagia, a single-nave basilica was built, but destroyed by fire in 1885.

In Greek, *agora* means "market" or "bazaar", and as you can guess, this site served

as such. It was a commercial, political and spiritual center where citizens gathered to shop, talk and worship. The Roman Agora was built in the first century BC with donations from Julius Caesar and Augustus. It was built in the Doric order and consisted of a large courtyard with colonnades on all four sides, shops, a fountain and a storeroom.

As you can see in the photos, there are two propylaias (entrance gates) to the Roman Agora. The monumental Doric column, Gate of Athena Archegetis (center photo), stands on the west side of the Agora. The other entrance gate (bottom photo) is on the eastern side and built in Ionic order.

The Tower of the Winds · Aerides

The Roman Agora is actually divided in two sections: lower and upper. The Tower of the Winds (*Horologion* meaning "timepiece") is one block away from Adrianou on Aeolou Street and is part of the ancient Roman Agora. It is the most impressive and well-preserved monument from the Roman period. It is debatable when the tower was built; some sources say about 100-50 BC, while others indicate that it was erected during the 2nd century BC before the rest of the Roman Forum. Built by the Syrian astronomer, Andronikos Kyrrhestes, the tower has served as a sundial, water clock (operated by water running down from the Acropolis) and weather vane. The octagonal tower is made out of Pentelic marble and stands on a base with three steps. As we look up at the tower, we can see that each of the eight sides is decorated with beautiful friezes representing the winds that blow from that direction. The rooftop of the monument is cone shaped and at one time it had a revolving weather vane depicting Triton.

During the early Christian period, the tower was used as a church, and during the 18th century it became a Turkish Dervish monastery.

We can also see one of the few remains of the Turkish occupation where the Fethiye Djami Mosque still stands. It was built in the 15th century AD on the site of a Christian church to celebrate the

Turkish conquest of Athens and to also honor Mehmet II the Conqueror. Today the Mosque is used as a storage house.
Hours: Summer 8:00 am-7:30 pm

The Medrese · Koranic Theological School

Across from the Tower of the Winds you will find the Medrese, the Koranic Theological School which was founded in 1721 by Mehmet Fahri. During the Greek War of Independence, the Turks used it as a prison and hung many Greek prisoners from a tree that was next to the building. After the Greek War of Independence, the Greeks used the building and tree for the same purpose. The people in the neighborhood believed that the tree was cursed and the poet Achilleas Paraschos predicted that one day the tree would be destroyed and used for firewood. And this is exactly what happened! In 1919, the tree was struck by lightning, chopped up, and used for firewood. Then the building was demolished. The door that you see today is the only part that remained.

Church of the Archangels & Virgin Mary Taxiarches & Panagia Grigorousa

Across from Hadrian's Library, at the corner of Dexippou and Taxiarches Streets, is the Church of the Archangels. Originally, a small church stood on the same site during the Byzantine period that was built during the 12th century. It was destroyed by a fire in 1832 and reconstructed in 1922. The current church is modern on the outside but traditional inside. It houses a miraculous icon of the Virgin Mary called the Grigorousa.

MELINA MERCOURI FOUNDATION

Odos: Polygnotou 9-11
Hours: Daily: 10:00 am - 2:00 pm; Closed Mondays

If you travel back south to Polygnotou street and turn right, you will arrive at the Melina Mercouri Foundation which was founded by Jules Dassin, Melina's husband. Its main purpose is to promote and perpetuate Melina's dream in raising money for the return of the Parthenon Marbles to the new Acropolis Museum.

HELPFUL GREEK WORDS

Η Ρωμαϊκή Αγορά • Ee Romayee<u>kee</u> Ag<u>or</u>a • The Roman Market

Η Βιβλιοθήκη του Ανδριανού • Ee Veevleeo<u>thee</u>kee tou Andreea<u>nou</u> • Hadrian's Library

Ο Τετράκχος Μεγάλη Παναγία • O Te<u>tra</u>khos Me<u>ga</u>lee Pana<u>yee</u>a • Tetraconch-Megali Panagia

Το Ωρολόγιο του Ανδρονίκου Κυρρήστου • To Oro<u>lo</u>geio tou Andro<u>nee</u>kou Kir<u>ree</u>stou • The Tower of the Winds

Ο Μεντρεσές • O Medre<u>ses</u> • The Medrese

Οι Ταξιάρχες Παναγία Γρηγορούσα • Ee Taksee<u>ar</u>hes Pana<u>yee</u>a Greego<u>rou</u>sa • Archangels & Virgin Mary-Taxiarches & Panagia Grigorousa

Το Ίδρυμα Μελίνα Μερκούρη • To <u>Ee</u>dreema Me<u>lee</u>na Mer<u>kou</u>ree • Melina Mercouri Foundation

THE ANCIENT AGORA

If you walk back to Adrianou Street and go west, you will be walking towards the entrance to the Ancient Agora. Before entering, you may want to visit St. Phillip church.

Agios Filippos · Saint Philip

Odos: Adrianou

St. Philip Church is situated on Adrianou Street, opposite to the entrance of the Ancient Agora. It was built in 1866 on the remains of an older church that was probably built in the 17th century. It is believed that Saint Philip spoke to the Athenians on this site.

Ancient Agora

The ancient agora, or marketplace, is a wide open space under the Acropolis. It is near the Thission Metro Station and near the Monastiraki flea market.

During the Neolithic period (3000 BC), the agora was used as a residential and burial area. In the 6th century BC, Peisistratos remodeled it by removing the houses, closing the well and adding a drainage system, fountains and a temple dedicated to the Olympian Gods. In the 5th century BC the temples of Hephaestos, Zeus and Apollo were built. Throughout time, new buildings (a royal palace, court house, and jail) were added to the Agora.

The Agora soon became the heart of ancient Athens - the center of the Athenian government and a public location where people met for economical, cultural, political and religious activities. It is at this very location where Socrates and Plato gathered to have discussions with their students. In fact, it is here were Socrates drank the hemlock! Imagine walking down the same paths where these famous philosophers and so many other important people walked... The Agora is also where the city's administrative and legislative buildings were located. The *Boule* (city council), the *Prytaneis* (presidents of the council), and archons/magistrates all gathered in the Agora. The law courts also met here and any citizen found in the Agora when a case was being heard could be forced to serve as a juror.

In 480 BC the Agora was extensively damaged by the Persians, but later, during the Roman and Byzantine times, it was restored as a residential area. Unfortunately, the Agora didn't remain in such condition and eventually vanished.

In the middle of the 19th century, the Greek Archaeological Society began the first excavations on the Agora. Both in 1896 &

1987, workers making big trenches for the Athens-Piraeus Railroad system found the remains of many famous buildings. In order to continue excavations in this area, over four hundred buildings had to be demolished. In 1931, the American School of Classical Studies initiated new excavations on the site which are still in process today. Much of the area is in ruins; however, there are a few incredible monuments that are still quite intact. Let me take you on a tour around this fabulous ancient marketplace.

Temple of Hephaestos

This is also known as the Temple of Thission. It was built in 449 BC and dedicated to the gods Hephaestos (the god of blacksmiths and metallurgy) and Athena (the goddess of wisdom), and designed by Iktinos, one of the architects that worked on the Parthenon. This Doric style temple has six columns in the front and thirteen on the side. It is the best preserved of all ancient Greek temples in the world, in which its columns, pediments and most of the roof is still intact. During the 7th century AD, the temple was converted to the church of St. George, which helped in its preservation. During the Ottoman occupation it served as the main church of Athens. When the first king of Greece, Otto, was welcomed to the city, his ceremony took place at this very site.

Stoa of Attalos

This stoa is considered to be one of the most remarkable buildings in the Agora. It was built by and named after King Attalos II of Pergamon, who ruled between 159 BC and 138 BC. The stoa, which is made of Pentelic marble and limestone, is comprised of different architectural orders. The exterior colonnade on the ground floor was made in Doric order while the interior colonnade used Ionic order.

The exterior colonnade of the first floor was Ionic. The temple was a gift to the Athenians from Attalos for the education that he received in Athens. The stoa was used until it was destroyed by the

Heruli in 267. The ruins were then used for a fortification wall. In 1940, the stoa was reconstructed and made into the Agora Museum. In this museum, you can see exhibits from the excavations of the Agora. The collections include sculpture, pottery, and lamps dating from the 4th century BC up through the Byzantine period and Turkish Domination.

In 2003, the signing of the Treaty of Accession of ten countries (Cyprus, the Czech Republic, Estonia, Latvia, Lithuania, Hungary, Malta, Poland, Slovakia and Slovenia) to the European Union took place here. I love walking around the stoa; there are so many magnificent statues, columns and plaques to discover.

ODEON OF AGRIPPA

Built by Agrippa (a Roman statesman and general) in 15 BC, the Odeon was a large concert hall in the center of the Agora. It was equipped with a raised stage and a marble-paved orchestra pit, and was decorated with Corinthian pilasters. The hall seated about 1,000 people. In 150 AD the roof collapsed and was later rebuilt into a smaller lecture hall that seated about 500 people. Massive pillars were carved in the form of giants and tritons. In 267 AD the Agora was destroyed by a fire and then in 400 AD a gymnasium was built in the area. Four colossal statues of giants and tritons on pedestals have survived the fire.

FOOTSTEPS THROUGH ATHINA

THE STATUE OF HADRIAN

This slightly larger than life statue of Roman Emperor Hadrian is found in the eastern section of the Agora. It is dedicated to the emperor who loved Greek culture and built many structures in Greece.

AGII APOSTOLOI SOLAKI
HOLY APOSTLES SOLAKI

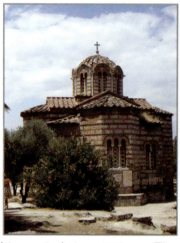

The church of the Holy Apostles Solaki is located on the south-eastern side of the Ancient Agora. Holy Apostles is a mid-Byzantine church from the 10th century and one of Athens' oldest churches. It was built over a circular *nymphaion* (sacred spring) and built in the cross-in-square form with a dome borne on four columns. The exterior has *Kufic* (Arabic script) inscriptions. The interior of the church is well preserved with frescoes of the Pantocrator of Christ, St. John the Baptist, cherubim and archangels.

HELPFUL GREEK WORDS

Ο ΄Αγιος Φίλιππος • O Ayeeos Feeleepos • Saint Philip

Η Αρχαία Αγορά • Ee Archea Agora • The Ancient Agora

Ο Ναός Ηφαίστου • O Naos Eefestou • Temple of Hephaestos

Η Στοά Αττάλου • Ee Stoa Attalou • Stoa of Attalos

Το Ωδείο Αγρίππα • To Odeeo Agreepa • The Odeio of Agrippa

Το ΄Αγαλμα Αδριανού • To Agalma Adrianou • Statue of Hadrian

Οι ΄Αγιοι Απόστολοι Σολάκη • Ee Ayee Apostolee Solakee • Holy Apostles Solaki

FOOTSTEPS THROUGH ATHINA

FOOTSTEPS THROUGH THE WESTERN NEIGHBORHOODS: PSIRRI

Psirri is located just north of Monastiraki and is surrounded by the streets Ermou, Athinas, Evripidou, Epikourou, Pireos and the archaeological site of Keramikos. You can easily reach it on foot from Keramikos and Monastiraki. Over the past few years, it has become a very popular place among young adults. In the evening, it is often so crowded that it is hard to circulate around the main streets. Let's check out some of the sites.

ELEFTHERIAS KOUMOUNDOUROU SQUARE

The popular Koumoundourou Square is in Psirri adjacent to Pireos Street. It was named after Alexandros Koumoundouros, who was prime minister several times during the rein of King George I. His house used to stand in this square. During the Ottoman Era, a

fortification wall was built around this area. Once Greece was freed, the wall was knocked down. In the 1990's, the square became the home to refugees who slept out in the open area. It suffered greatly from deterioration until the unification project of Athens renovated the square and also acquired several new plants and trees. It has become a favorite spot among Athenians who visit the shops, art galleries, and restaurants in the neighborhood and also among skateboarders who love the large open space. You can find a lot of Chinese restaurants here too.

Agii Anargyroi
Saints Anargyri
Poor or Penniless Saints

Odos: Eleftherias Koumoundourou Square

This church is situated in the northeast corner of the square. It was built over an older Byzantine church in 1827 that the Ottoman army destroyed when they besieged the Acropolis. The Byzantine style church (cross-in-square type) of Agii Anargyroi was rebuilt in 1832.

Athens Municipal Gallery of Athens

Odos: Panagi Tsaldari Street
Hours: Daily: 9:00 am - 1:00 pm and
5:00 pm - 9:00 pm
Weekends: Closed

The Municipal Gallery of Athens is housed in a neoclassical building and located in Koumoundourou Square. Inaugurated in 1982, the gallery features a fabulous

FOOTSTEPS THROUGH ATHINA

collection of about 2,500 works of art (engravings, paintings and drawings) mostly by 20th century Greek artists such as Georgios Iakovidis, Konstantinos Parthenis, Georgios Bouzianis, Georgios Gounaropoulos, Nikos Engonopoulos, Giannis Moralis, Spiros Papoulakis and others. In addition, you can view the collection of architectural and historical works by the famous architects Ziller and Hansen who built so many of the beautiful neoclassical buildings in Athens.

BENAKI MUSEUM OF ISLAMIC ART

Odos: 22 Assomaton & 12 Dipliou
Hours: Tuesday & Thursday - Saturday: 9:00 am - 3:00 pm
Wednesday: 9:00 am - 9:00 pm

The Museum of Islamic Art is a branch of the Benaki Museum and is situated in a neoclassical building in the district of Kerameikos. It houses the superb Islamic art collection of Antonis Benakis with over 10,000 works of art originating from India, Persia, Mesopotamia, Asia Minor, the Middle East, Arabia, Egypt, North Africa, Sicily and Spain. The collection represents Islamic Art from the evolution of the Islamic civilization up to the Ottoman Empire (19th century). The Islamic Art Museum is considered to be one of the best in the world.

HELPFUL GREEK WORDS

Η Ψυρρή • Ee Pseerri • Psirri
Η Πλατεία Ελευθερίας Κουμουντούρου • Ee Plateea Eleforthereeas Koumoundourou • Eleftherias Koumoundourou Square
Οι ´Αγιοι Ανάργυροι • Ee Ayee Anaryeeree • Saints Anargyroi
Η Δημοτική Γαλερί της Αθήνας • Ee Deemotikee Galleree tees Atheenas • Athens Municipal Gallery of Athens
Το Μπενάκη Μουσείο της Ισλαμικής Τέχνης • To Benakee Mouseeo tees Eeslameekees Teknees • Benaki Museum of Islamic Art

THE WESTERN NEIGHBORHOODS: PSIRRI, KERAMIKOS, GAZI, THISSION

FOOTSTEPS THROUGH ATHINA

KERAMIKOS

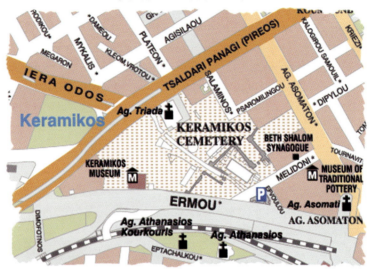

AGII ASSOMATI • HOLY APOSTLES
Odos: Ermou & Asomaton Streets

This small church dates back to the first half of the 11th century (around 1020). It is the oldest Byzantine church in Athens today. Holy Apostles was built with the typical characteristics of a Byzantine church from this period: a large dome supported by four columns, cross-in-square form and sculptured stone surrounded by brick. It does differ, however, from other churches in that the central space is surrounded by four apses and four apsidioles, giving it two extra rooms at both ends.

MUSEUM OF TRADITIONAL POTTERY
Odos: 4-6 Melidoni

It is very appropriate that a pottery museum be situated in the area of Keramikos, the place where ancient potters had their

workshops. Created by the Georgios Psaropoulos Family Foundation, the museum is located in a 19th century mansion and houses over 4,500 ceramic works from the last three centuries. While here, you can view reconstructions of pottery workshops, videos, photos, and also visit the library, museum shop or café.

Beth Shalom Synagogue
House of Peace Jewish Synagogue
Odos: 5 Melidoni - Jewish Quarter
Etz Hayim Synagogue
Odos: 8 Melidoni - Jewish Quarter

You might be wondering why there are two synagogues in this area. Before the Second World War, this was Athens' biggest and most vibrant Jewish Quarter (Evraika) where over 3,000 Jews resided. Etz Hayim is the oldest synagogue in Athens. It was originally built by the Romaniote Jews (Jews from Ioannina) in 1903. Situated in a white two-story stucco building, the synagogue is often referred to as the Ioanniotiki

Synagogue. Today, it is used only for High Holiday Services and special occasions.

Across the street, you will find the Beth Shalom Synagogue, built in the 1930's to meet the needs of the expanding community of Jewish refugees from Asia Minor. The synagogue is housed in a beautiful neoclassical building made of Pentelic marble. It was remodeled in 1975 because it suffered much damage during World War II.

Keramikos Cemetery

Heading southwest on Melidoni, there is an open pedestrian walk. Turn right and head for Keramikos Cemetery. This is a cemetery where the most important ancient Athenians were buried from the 9th century BC until the late Roman period. Even though Keramikos Cemetery is considered to be a classical masterpiece, it is unfortunately unknown to many visitors and remains one of the least visited archaeological sites in Athens.

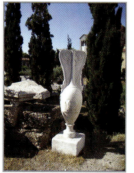

Keramikos was named after a community of potters (called *keramis* in Greek) who worked within the inner gates and occupied the whole area along the banks of the Eridanos River (a small river that once passed through Athens and still flows beneath the site). The area had very good clay that the potters used to make ceramics.

While walking around the cemetery, you will notice the remains of the first ancient city walls built in the 5th century BC by Themistocles. The walls divided the area into two sections: inner and outer Keramikos. The cemetery was located outside of the city

walls. The areas were connected by two gates placed at the onset of the two most important processional roads of Athens. One gate was the Dipylon Gate (double gateway), the main entrance into Athens.

FOOTSTEPS THROUGH ATHINA

The roads from Piraeus, Thebes, Corinth and the Peloponnese all led to this gate. The Dipylon was the largest gate in ancient Greece. It was also the most important gate because the Panathenaic procession leading to the Parthenon began here. The other gate is called the Sacred Gate. It was reserved for priestesses to pass on to the Sacred Road to Eleusis. It is also at this point that the Eridanos River passed through. The remains of these gates are still visible today.

At one point, a spacious building with a courtyard called the Pompeion stood between these two gates. It was used to store the equipment for the Panathenaic procession and was also the spot where the processions started and where all those involved in the festivities would prepare for the event. The church of Agia Triada (left) stands in the background.

As you stroll around the Street of the Tombs (near the Sacred Gate), you will encounter tombstones where the wealthy Athenians were buried. The remarkable sculptured tombs standing under an array of cedar trees display depictions of scenes from mythology and relief portrayals of the deceased. In 317 BC, Demetrios Falireos, the governor of Athens, issued a decree that forbid placing large monuments in the cemetery. From this point on, people used small columns called *kioniski* (right). The names and birthplaces of the deceased were written on these columns. You can locate them near the museum, which is the next place to visit.

THE WESTERN NEIGHBORHOODS: PSIRRI, KERAMIKOS, GAZI, THISSION

FOOTSTEPS THROUGH ATHINA

THE KERAMEIKOS ARCHAEOLOGICAL MUSEUM

Odos: 8 Ermou
Hours: Tuesday - Sunday: 8:30 am - 7:30 pm

The museum of Keramikos houses a large collection of vases, statues, grave steles and pottery from the cemetery. It was built in 1937 by H. Johannes with a donation by Gustav Oberlaender and enlarged in the 1960's with the financial help of the Boehringer brothers. Most recent finds can be found in this museum, whereas the older objects are housed in the National Archaeological Museum.

HELPFUL GREEK WORDS

Ο Κεραμεικός • O Kerameekos • Kerameikos

Οι΄Αγιοι Ασώματοι • Ee Ayee Asomatee • Holy Apostles

Το Μουσείο Νεώτερης Κεραμικής • To Mouseeo Neoterees Kerameekees • The Museum of Traditional Pottery

Η Εβραϊκή Συναγώγη • Ee Evrayeekee Seenagogee • The Jewish Synagogue

Οι Ρωμανιώτες Εβραίοι • Ee Romaneeotes Evrayee • The Romaniote Jews

Το Αρχαιολογικό Μουσείο Κεραμεικού • To Arhelogeeko Mouseeo Kerameekou • The Archaeological Kerameikos Museum

FOOTSTEPS THROUGH ATHINA

GAZI

Gazi is located just west of Keramikos. This neighborhood was named Gazi because there was once a gas factory with the same name. The entire area consisted of beautiful neoclassical buildings made of stone with wooden roofs and skylights. In addition, many of the buildings also contained French and Byzantine tiles on their edifices. The district of Gazi has recently been restored and renovated and the area now serves as an industrial park. The neighborhood also boasts numerous restaurants and nightclubs.

GAZI · CITY OF ATHENS TECHNOPOLIS GAZI FACTORY WORKSHOPS

Odos: Pireos 100
Hours: Daily: 10:00 am - 10:00 pm

The Gazi factory was established in 1857 and began functioning in 1862. It closed down in 1984 and is known to be the last factory in Europe that was operated in a traditional way. Since 1999, the City of Athens Technopolis has been serving as an industrial museum and a multi-purpose cultural center. It is dedicated to the memory of the famous Greek composer Manos Hatzidakis. The eight buildings within the Technopolis bear the names of great Greek poets

(Andreas Embirikos, Angelos Sikelianos, Yannis Ritsos, Kostis Palamis, Takis Paptsonis, Constantine Cavafy and Kostas Varnalis).

Maria Callas Museum

Odos: Pireos 100
Hours: Tuesday - Friday: 9:00 am - 1:00 pm & 5:00 pm - 9:00 pm
Sunday: 9:00 am - 1:00 pm

The Maria Callas Museum has been housed in the City of Athens Technopolis (Andreas Embirikos Hall) since 2002. It pays tribute to the greatest female opera soprano of the 20th century and presents a fine collection of her letters, photos and pieces of her wardrobe.

HELPFUL GREEK WORDS
Το Γκάζι • To Gazee • Gazi
Η Τεχνόπολη • Ee Technopolee • Technopolis
Η Μαρία Κάλλας • Ee Mareea Kallas • Maria Kallas

FOOTSTEPS THROUGH ATHINA

THISSION

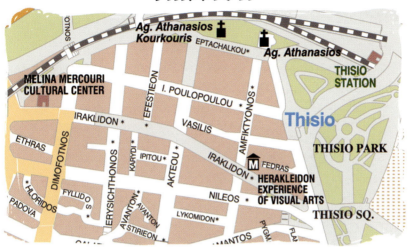

THE WESTERN NEIGHBORHOODS: PSIRRI, KERAMIKOS, GAZI, THISSION

Thission is next to Monastiraki, under the Acropolis. The area took its name from Thissio, the Temple of Hephaestos. To reach Thission from Gazi, head southeast.

This section boasts great restaurants, cafeterias (that the young people love), snack bars and museums. In addition to visiting the new establishments that have recently popped up here, you should also check out the many landmarks, buildings and historical squares that add to the significance of this district.

AGIOS/SAINT ATHANASSIOS KOURKOURIS

Odos: Eptachalkou Street

Saint Athanassios Kourkouris is a small white chapel that sits upon a rock on what was once the site of an ancient monument. The island style church built in the post-Byzantine period was named after its owner Kourkouris. It is situated on the pedestrian Eptachalkou Street.

127

FOOTSTEPS THROUGH ATHINA

AGIOS ATHANASSIOS ATHONITIS
SAINT ATHANASSIOS THE ATHONITE

Odos: Eptachalkou Street

Next to the chapel on the eastern side is the church of Saint Athanassios Athonitis. Built in 1756 in this old Turkish section of Thission, it has a very impressive marble entrance and bell tower.

MELINA MERCOURI CULTURAL CENTER OF ATHENS

Odos: 66 Iraklidon Street
Hours: Tuesday - Saturday: 9:00 am – 1:00 pm & 5:00 pm - 9:00 pm
Sun: 9:00 am - 1:00 pm

This building is the former Poulopoulos Hat Factory, founded by Ilias Poulopoulos in 1886. Ilias was a very successful Greek businessman and many of his hats won international prizes. The factory functioned until the middle of the 20th

Footsteps Through Athina

century. In 1985, the building was recognized by the Greek government as a landmark monument. Although only a small portion of the building remained intact, the interesting stonework on it reflects the industrial architecture of that era. The building was restored and today serves as the Melina Mercouri Cultural Center. Upon visiting, one can catch a glimpse of what Athens was like during the 19th century on the upper floor of the center. You can walk along a reconstructed Athens street filled with neoclassical homes, a pharmacy, printing press, dry goods store, kafeneio and a dress shop.

Herakleidon Experience of Visual Arts

Odos: 16 Herakleidon Street
Hours: Tuesday - Saturday: 1:00 pm - 9:00 pm
Sunday: 11:00 am - 7:00 pm
Monday: Closed

This new museum is housed in a neoclassical building that dates back to 1898. It is situated on Herakleidon Street, aligned with the Acropolis. The Herakleidon Museum collection consists of Greek and foreign artists who play or have played an important role in the evolution of art. Mr. Paul Firos and his wife, Anna-Belinda, were inspired to create this museum due to their love of art and neoclassical buildings. Their goal is to present the evolution and technique of art. The museum also exhibits sketches, drawings, photographs and personal items belonging to the artists. The museum features wonderful exhibitions such as that of Toulouse-Lautrec. In addition to offering an array of educational school programs, Herakleidon also has a great museum shop with an online catalogue.

While on this street, you will notice many cafés and restaurants that are almost always filled with people. These establishments are quite lively both days and evenings. At the end

FOOTSTEPS THROUGH ATHINA

of Herakleidon Street at Thission Square is Apostolou Pavlou pedestrian street which is also lined with more cafés and restaurants, nestled among the neoclassical buildings and views of the Ancient Agora and Acropolis.

HELPFUL GREEK WORDS

Το Θησείο • To Thee<u>see</u>o • To Thission
Ο ΄Αγιος Αθανάσιος Κουρκούρης • O <u>A</u>yios Atha<u>na</u>seeos Kour<u>kou</u>rees • Saint Athanassios Kourkouris
Ο ΄Αγιος Αθανάσιος ο Αθωνίτης • O <u>A</u>yios Atha<u>na</u>seeos o Atho<u>nee</u>tees • St. Anathasios the Athonite
Το Πολιτιστικό Κέντρο Αθηνών Μελίνα Μερκούρη • To Poleeteestee<u>ko</u> <u>Ken</u>dro Athee<u>non</u>-Me<u>lee</u>na Mer<u>kou</u>ree • Melina Mercouri Cultural Center of Athens
Το Μουσείο Καλών Τέχνων Herakleidon • To Mous<u>ee</u>oo Ka<u>lon</u> <u>Tek</u>non Herakl<u>ei</u>don • Herakleidon Experience of Visual Arts

FOOTSTEPS THROUGH VASILISSIS SOFIAS AND KOLONAKI

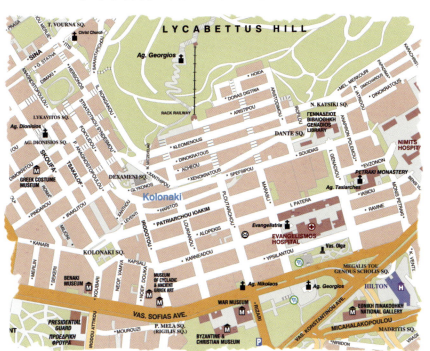

We are back in front of the Parliament and will now take a walk down Vasilissis Sofias Avenue. The avenue, named after the former queen of Greece, begins at the intersections of Amalias Avenue and Panepistimiou Street and ends at Alexandras, Kiffisias and Mesogeion Streets. At Vasilissis Sofias Avenue we will turn right (east) and proceed down this elegant boulevard lined with neoclassical buildings - many of which are museums and embassies.

Benaki Museum

Odos: Vas. Sofias Avenue & 1 Koumbari Street
Hours: Monday, Wednesday, Friday, Saturday: 9:00 am – 5:00 pm
Thursday: 9:00 am – 12:00 Midnight
Sunday: 9:00 am – 3:00 pm

The beautiful, neoclassical Benaki Museum was originally the home of Emmanouil Benakis, a wealthy merchant from Alexandria. In 1929, his son Antonis Benakis founded the first museum in Greece to house his many collections that were eventually donated to the Greek State. Today the museum exhibits over 40,000 items including: icons, oil paintings and wood carvings, historical archives, ceramics, metalworks, glass and bone artifacts, textiles and photography. As you view these beautiful works of art, you can travel through the various historical periods of Greece beginning with antiquity, up to the present day. Make sure that you allow a lot of time to see it all!

Nikos Hadjikyriakos · Ghikas Gallery

Odos: Same building as the Benaki Museum
Hours: Monday, Wednesday, Friday, Saturday: 9:00 am – 5:00 pm
Thursday: 9:00 am – 12:00 Midnight
Sunday: 9:00 am – 3:00 pm

Opening in 2009, this gallery is a branch of the Benaki Museum. It houses the paintings and artworks of Nikos Hadjikyriakos-Ghikas, a leading figure in Modern Greek art. Ghikas was influenced by cubism and his works can be admired in the most important museums throughout the world today. In the 1930's, Ghikas served as a professor at the Athens Technical University. He donated his house to the Benaki museum. Ghikas designed the gallery which opened in 1991, three years before his death.

FOOTSTEPS THROUGH ATHINA

Museum of Cycladic Art

Odos: Vas. Sofias Avenue & 1 Irodotou Street
Hours: Monday-Wednesday-Thursday-Friday: 10:00 am - 4:00 pm
Saturday: 10:00 am - 3:00 pm

The Museum of Cycladic Art is the perfect place to learn all about prehistoric and ancient Greek art. Founded in 1986 to house the collections of Nicholas and Dolly Goulandris, this museum has one of the finest collections in the world of Cycladic Art (artifacts made on the Cycladic Greek islands) dating back from 3200 BC to 2000 BC. At this time, the small islands in the Aegean became home of a flourishing civilization. The art was mainly revealed in marble; human-form idols often used as offerings to the dead. The majority of the figures show women with their hands folded over their stomach. The museum consists of two buildings; the modern building where the permanent collection is displayed and the extension featuring temporary exhibitions. Don't forget to visit the gift shop where you can pick up a reproduction of the marvelous white statues.

Byzantine and Christian Museum

Odos: Vas. Sofias 22
Hours: Tues - Sun: 8:00 am - 7:30 pm

After visiting the numerous Byzantine churches in Plaka and having been exposed to so many beautiful icons, you may want to devote more time learning about the Byzantine era (4th to 15th century AD) of Greece. As you can probably tell from its name, this Museum concentrates exclusively on Byzantine art. Built in 1914, the museum displays a collection of over 25,000 icons, tapestries, mosaics, church vestments, Bibles, and a small-scale, reconstructed

VASILISSIS SOFIAS AND KOLONAKI

early Christian basilica. The museum has a museum shop where you can find books, icons and CDs of Byzantine music.

War Museum
Odos: Vas. Sofias 2 & Rizeri
Hours: Tuesday - Saturday: 9:00 am - 2:00 pm

Inaugurated in 1975, the War Museum stands out from the many neoclassical buildings on this street as it is constructed in a late modernism style and has a quite peculiar shape. Actually, this building was built during the Junta Military Dictatorship and has been criticized by many for its architecture. As you can see in the photo, the first floor of the building is bigger than the ground floor. You will have no problem finding it - just look for the war planes (you can actually climb into the cockpit of a fighter plane), cannons, and statues that are surrounding the building. Upon your visit, you can view many war mementos and learn about the thousands of years of Greek war history, dating from pre-historic times until today. You will find great collections of weapons: primitive ones used during the Stone Age, as well as the early Bronze Age.

St. Nicholas of the Poorhouse
Odos: Vas. Sofias

This late 19th century Neo-Byzantine church is directly across the street from the War Museum and stands in front of the British Embassy. Built in 1876 by Panayiotis Kalkos, the church contains irregular stonework and is accented with two color brickwork. It was built in the Byzantine style during the era of Neoclassicism.

FOOTSTEPS THROUGH ATHINA

EVANGELISMOS METRO STATION

The Evangelismos Metro Station is located on Vas. Sofia and is situated across the street from the Evangelismos General Hospital. Here is another train station that has a great display of antiquities in an open air museum next to the entrance. The exhibition includes ancient graves, fragments of the Pisistratid aqueduct and a Roman era potters kiln.

CHURCH OF ST. GEORGE RIZARIS ECCLESIASTICAL SCHOOL

Odos: 51 Vas.Sofias

This neoclassical church was built in 1843 and funded by George Rizaris, a merchant and national benefactor of Greece. He also established the Rizaris Ecclesiastical School which recently moved to the nearby suburb of Halandri. Today, the building houses the administrative offices of the school. A bust of George Rizaris is in the entrance to the church.

SQUARE OF THE GREAT SCHOOL OF THE NATION · THE RUNNER STATUE

Odos: Vas. Sofias & Vas. Konstantinou

As we continue down Vas. Sofias we will arrive at the intersection where Vas. Konstantinou meets this street. We are now at a triangular green square which is called Square of the Great School of the Nation. It is named after a boys high school/college in Constantinople that was founded by the Patriachiate. The square contains *The Runner*, a colossal striding, impressionist statue constructed of large slabs of horizontally-stacked broken glass. It was designed in 1988 by Costas Varotsas and originally stood in Omonia Square. In 1994, it was moved to this spot due to the construction of the Metro there and has remained here since. It was placed in a perfect spot since this is the direction to the 2004 Olympic Stadium and village.

National Art Gallery
Alexandros Soutzos Museum
National Pinakotheki

Odos: 50 Vassileos Konstantinou Avenue & 1 Michalakopoulou
Hours: Monday - Saturday: 9:00 am - 3:00 pm
Sunday: 10:00 am - 2:00 pm
Tuesday: Closed

Now let's cross the street and visit the National Art Gallery, or Alexandros Soutzos Museum - the most important and complete Greek institution devoted to the history of Greek art. The Art Gallery was founded in 1900 and, at this time, the famous Greek painter, Georgios Iakovidis, was appointed as the first curator. The gallery was then comprised of 258 works from the collections of the University of Athens and the Technical University of Athens. One year later, Alexandros Soutzos added to this by

donating his collection of 107 paintings. In 1964, with the help of donations from art lovers and artists, the current building was completed and inauguarated. Today, the museum houses more than 15,000 paintings, sculptures, engravings and other forms of art from the post-Byzantine period up until today. It boasts a very fine gift shop where you can pick up great souvenirs for your art-appreciating friends back home.

Footsteps Through Athina

Hilton Hotel • A Landmark

Odos: 46 Vas. Sofias

The Hilton Hotel is a landmark of Athens. It was built in 1963 and recently remodeled for the Athens 2004 Olympics. The hotel features 524 spacious rooms, all with a great view from the balcony. There are three restaurants, with the Byzantine Restaurant being a favorite among Athenians for coffee or lunch, and the place to eat American food if you really miss it! The Hilton also has a great outdoor swimming pool and a number of other amenities.

Eleftherios Venizelos Museum & Park

Past the Hilton on the left hand side of the street, you will approach this spacious, green park; something a bit rare to find in Athens since it is a very dry city, and also limited in free space. It is called Eleftherios Venizelos Park and was named after the great politician and one of Europe's most charismatic leaders of his time. Venizelos was born in Crete. He was the founder of the Liberal Party and served as Prime Minister of Greece during the Balkan Wars (1912-1913), WWI (1914-1918), and the Asia Minor War (1919-1922). He is considered one of the most significant politicians of modern Greece and as you probably noticed, the new airport has been named after him. As you are walking around the park you will find his statue.

The park was developed in the 1960's on a piece of land where bitter memories of Greece's turbulent historical past are buried. The building complex behind the park was used by the 34th regiment during the Balkan War era. This is where Venizelos would address his soldiers before they went off to war. During the Junta Military Dictatorship (1967-1974), these buildings were used by the military police to question and torture opponents of the regime.

There are a few museums to visit in this park: The Eleftherios Museum, founded in 1986, which displays personal items and documents of Venizelos; the Athens Municpality Arts Centre, used for temporary exhibits and seminars; and an Anti-Dictatorial & Democratic Resistance Museum.

Megaron Mousikis Concert Hall

Just past the park is Megaron Mousikis Concert Hall, a beautifully designed building that was completed in 1991. Some of the best European consultants and companies were brought to Greece to create this hall that is today considered to be one of the  world's finest cultural centers; it also has a reputation for its superb acoustics. You can find a wide range of classical music programs here including quartets, operas in concerts, symphonies and ballet recitals. If you have the chance to attend, you will certainly enjoy the concerts! Unfortunately, very few events take place during the summer.

Agii Assomati Taxiarches Moni Petraki-Petrakis Monastery

Odos: Monis Street & 14 Gennadiou

The Petrakis Monastery and Church are situated behind the Evangelismos Hospital. Its entrance is on 14 Gennadiou Street. There are no records of when the

buildings of this complex were built; however, the bricks used in construction date back to the 10th-11th century. The main church is one of the oldest and most important in Athens. The octagonal dome dates back to the later Byzantine era (1204-1453). Only three semi-circular apses remain from the original church. The outer narthex was added during the 19th century. The monastery has witnessed several wars throughout Greece's history and has served several functions. It was plundered by the Ottomans during the Greek War of Independence. For a while after the war, it was used a national military hospital. During the Balkan Wars, it was used again by the Greek army and then after 1922, it housed Greek refugees from Turkey. During the German Occupation of World War II, Sunday meals were provided for needy children here.

Lycavittos Hill

Lycavittos Hill (Hill of the Wolves) is the highest hill in Athens and can be reached either by foot (it is a steep, twenty minute walk), taxi or by taking the funicular from Dexameni Street in Kolonaki. The view at the top is breathtaking with an incredible panorama of Athens; try to go at sunset and watch the magnificent colors of the sun shining upon the city! On a clear day, you can see most of central Attica, the Saronic Gulf with its northern islands and the northwestern Peloponnese. Don't forget to visit the little chapel of St. George located on top of the hill. It is also dedicated to the Prophet Elias and St. Constantine. There is a huge bell tower next to the chapel that was donated by Queen Olga. On the western, lower side of the hill, there are two cannons that are used on holidays and special occasions. This is a popular spot for Greeks to attend the Easter Resurrection Service. The entire hill is illuminated as the people descend the stairs with their burning candles at midnight. What a beautiful scene! If you are lucky, you can attend a concert in the open air theater; another fabulous experience. You can also stop for a snack at the outdoor coffee bar (a bit expensive) or if you are searching for a very good restaurant, Lycavittos has a great one (but again very expensive).

DISTRICT OF KOLONAKI

After leaving the Lycavittos Hill, we will walk over to the *Kolonaki* (little column) district - a wealthy, upscale neighborhood of Athens which is on the lower, southwestern slopes of Lycavittos Hill. As soon as we turn down Koumbari Street, we will hit Kolonaki Square, or Plateia Philikis Etaireias, as it was originally called. The name stands for a Greek society in Russia composed of diaspora Greeks that promoted Greece's liberation from the Ottoman Occupation. This is a fun place to stop for ice cream and to watch the chic Athenians dashing in and out of the many fabulous boutiques, galleries, cafés and restaurants. Who knows... you may even spot a famous person! You will notice several embassies in this area.

FOOTSTEPS THROUGH ATHINA

Agios Dionysios Areopagitis

Odos: 34 Skoufa

Agios Dionysios is dedicated to the first bishop and patron saint of Athens. Its masonry and decoration combine elements from various periods of church building, making it a truly impressive looking church. You will recognize it by its cross in shape form and big dome. Several prominent wealthy families donated icons for this church, adding to its beautiful interior that is decorated with mosaics and marble. The church was built after the Asia Minor Disaster of 1922. Originally, there was a smaller church on the same site that was demolished since it was too small to accommodate the needs of a growing population.

Museum of the History of Greek Costume

Odos: 7 Dimokritou
Hours: Monday - Wednesday - Friday: 10:00 am - 1:00 pm

Founded in 1989, this museum is part of the Lyceum Club of Greek Women. In 1910, the members of this club began to collect costumes from all over Greece. Today the collection includes over 25,000 items of costumes, jewelry and dolls dressed in costumes, representing the Minoan, Archaic and Byzantine periods of Greek history.

VASILISSIS SOFIAS AND KOLONAKI

Footsteps Through Athina

HELPFUL GREEK WORDS

Το Μουσείο Μπενάκη • To Mou<u>see</u>o Be<u>na</u>kee • Benaki Museum

Το Κτήριο Πινακοθήκης του Χατζηκυριάκου Γκίκα • To <u>kteer</u>eeo Peenako<u>thee</u>kees tou Hadzeekeeree<u>a</u>kou <u>Gee</u>ka • Nikos Hadjikyriakos-Ghikas Gallery

Το Μουσείο Κυκλαδικής Τέχνης • To Mou<u>see</u>o Keekladi<u>kees</u> <u>Tech</u>nees • Museum of Cycladic Art

Το Βυζαντινό και Χριστανικό Μουσείο • To Veezantee<u>no</u> ke Chreestanee<u>ko</u> Mou<u>see</u>o • The Byzantine & Christian Museum

Το Πολεμικό Μουσείο • To Polemee<u>ko</u> Mou<u>see</u>o • The War Museum

Ο Άγιος Νικόλαος • O <u>A</u>yeeos Neeko<u>la</u>os • St. Nicholas

Ο Ευαγγελισμός Σταθμός Μετρό • O Evangelees<u>mos</u> Stath<u>mos</u> <u>Me</u>tro • The Evangelismos Metro Station

Η Ριζάρειος Εκκλησιαστική Σχολή • Ee Ree<u>za</u>reeos Ekleeseeastee<u>kee</u> Scho<u>lee</u> • Rizarios Ecclesiastical School

Ο Δρομέας • O Dro<u>me</u>as • The Runner

Η Εθνική Πινακοθήκη Μουσείο Αλέξανδρου Σούτζου • Ee Ethnee<u>kee</u> Peenako<u>thee</u>kee Mou<u>see</u>o A<u>lek</u>sandrou <u>Sout</u>zou • National Art Gallery Alexandros Soutzos

Το Ξενοδοχείο Χίλτον • To Ksenodo<u>hee</u>o <u>Heel</u>ton • The Hilton Hotel

Ο Ελευθέριος Βενιζέλος • O Elef<u>the</u>reeos Veenee<u>ze</u>los • Eleftherios Venizelos

Το Μέγαρον Μουσικής Αθηνών • To <u>Me</u>garon Mousee<u>kees</u> Athee<u>non</u> • The Megaron Mousikis Concert Hall

Οι Άγιοι Ασώματοι Ταξιάρχες • Ee <u>A</u>yee A<u>so</u>matee Taksee<u>ar</u>hes • Saints Assomati Taxiarches

Ο Λυκαβητός • O Leeka<u>vee</u>tos • Lycavittos

Το Κολωνάκι • To Kolo<u>na</u>kee • Kolonaki

Ο Άγιος Διονύσιος Αρεοπαγίτης • O <u>A</u>yeeos Deeo<u>nee</u>seeos Areopa<u>gee</u>tees • Agios Dionysios Areopagitis

Το Μουσείο Ιστορίας της Ελληνικής Ενδυμασίας • To Mou<u>see</u>o Eesto<u>ree</u>as tees Elleenee<u>kees</u> Entheema<u>see</u>as • The Museum of the History of Greek Costume

FOOTSTEPS THROUGH ATHINA

FOOTSTEPS AROUND THE UNIVERSITY

UNIVERSITY AREA AND STADIOU STREET

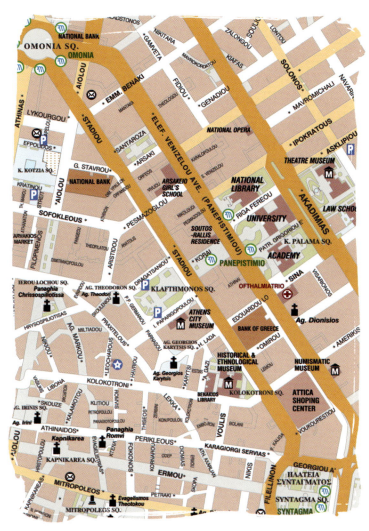

Once again we find ourselves in Syntagma Square. This time we will walk down the one way street called Eleftheriou Venizelou - Panepistimiou (University). It is one of the main avenues that connects Omonia Square to Syntagma Square. The street is named Eleftheriou Venizelou Street and it is still referred as this on street signs; but, being that this is where the first university was built (in Greece, the Balkans and the Eastern Mediterranean), most Athenians and maps refer to it as the Street of the University. It is lined with beautiful neoclassical buildings that were built in the 19th century, shortly after Greece gained independence. Three buildings comprise what is called the Neoclassical Trilogy. We will learn more about them as we get closer to the site.

Iliou Melathron Numismatic Museum

Odos: 12 Panepistimiou (El. Venizelou)
Hours: Tuesday-Sunday: 8:30am-3:00pm

This Numismatic Museum is housed in the Ilion Melathron (Palace of the Lion). It was originally the house of the famous German archaeologist, Heinrich Schliemann (1822-1890), who excavated Troy and Mycenae. The renaissance styled neoclassical building was built between 1870 & 1881 by the famous German architect, Ernst Ziller. It is one of his most famous works. Here are excellent collections of coins, medals and precious stones from ancient and modern Greece, Rome, the Byzantine Empire, the orient, medieval and modern Europe and the United States. In addition, you can admire the magnificent wall painted scenes of Pompeii.

Agios Dionysios Catholic Cathedral of Athens

Odos: 24 Panespistimiou (El. Venizelou)

After leaving the Numismatic Museum, we can cross Omirou Street and immediately, on our right, we will see Agios Dionysios Catholic Cathedral. The church was designed by Lysandros Kaftantzoglou (he designed a number of buildings on this block) in 1865 and its style is a combination of Renaissance, early Christian and Neoclassical elements. The porch is surrounded with pillars and marble stairs. Check out the beautiful stained glass windows that were made in Germany.

Athens Ophthalmology Eye Clinic
Odos: 26 Panepistimiou (El. Venizelou)

This next building, known as the Eye Clinic, was also designed by Lysandros Kaftantzoglou. You will notice that it has a stone façade with horizontal bricks and arched openings, and it is a bit different than the other buildings on the street. That is because it was built in a neo-Byzantine style and not neoclassical. The clinic opened up in 1854 and still operates as an eye hospital today.

The Academy of Athens
Odos: 28 Panepistimiou (El. Venizelou)

The graceful Academy, designed by the famous Danish architect Theofilos Hansen, is considered to be his most prestigious work. Built between 1859 and 1885, the building boasts a grand entrance with Ionian style columns and two lateral wings attached to the main building. It is adorned with a frieze depicting Greek mythology and also Greek sculptures.

FOOTSTEPS THROUGH ATHINA

THE ATHENS UNIVERSITY

Odos: 30 Panepistimiou (El. Venizelou)

The National and Kapodistrian University of Athens is situated between the Academy of Athens and the National Library. It was founded in 1837 and was originally housed on the northeast side of the Acropolis, in the residence of architect Stamatis Kleanthes. It was the first university in Greece, the Balkans and the eastern Mediterranean. In 1841, the university moved to its present site. The building was designed by the Danish architect Christian Hansen (Theofilos' brother). It consists of a group of buildings that form a "T" shape. The Ionian-style university entrance is embraced by columns and capitals that are perfect replicas of those found in the Propylaia of the Acropolis. A beautiful façade with magnificent wall paintings representing the birth of sciences in Greece is featured at the top of the entrance. Today the building serves as headquarters of the University of Athens and houses the offices of the rectorate, the judicial department, the archives and a ceremonial hall used for official university ceremonies.

THE NATIONAL LIBRARY

Odos: 32 Panepistimiou (El. Venizelou)

The National Library consists of three sections. The middle section is the biggest and houses the reading room. To enter, you must ascend the Renaissance styled, winding staircase and pass through the Doric-style row of columns that were modeled after the temple of Hephaestos in the Ancient Agora of

Thission. The reading room is covered by a glass ceiling. Built between 1887 and 1902, the library was designed by Christian Hansen, (the same architect who designed the university) and supervised by Ernst Ziller. Today, this building still houses the most comprehensive public library of Greece.

Theatre Museum

Odos: 50 Akadimias Street
Hours: Sunday-Friday: 10:00am – 2:30pm

For all of you theatre lovers, this is the place for you! It is located behind the University and across Akadimias Street. This museum was founded in 1938 by the Greek Theatre Writers Society. Since 1977, it has been housed in the basement of the Cultural Centre of the City of Athens. The museum has an extensive collection of photographs, playbills from the 19th and 20th centuries, theatrical sets and costumes, show memorabilia and personal items of great actors. They are displayed according to modern Greek theatre, opera, musical theatre, ancient Greek drama and puppet theatre. The museum also has an extensive library.

Arsakeio Girls' School

Odos: 47-49 Panepistimiou & Pesmazoglou

The Arsakeio Girls' School is another landmark on this street. It was designed by Lysandros Kaftantzoglou, a humanist architect and professor of the School of Arts. It was established in 1836 with funding from Apostolos Arsakis. The lot on which it was built was purchased through a nationwide fundraising campaign. The original plans were drawn up by Stamatis Kleanthis, but in the end Kaftantzoglou's design was preferred since it consisted of a two story building with a façade inscribed in a square, two interior courtyards and a church.

Stoa tou Vivliou • Book Arcade

Odos: 5 Pesmazoglou

Once you are in the Arsakeio building, you can visit the book arcade that was established in 1996 by the Society of the Friends of Education (Philekpedeftiki Etairia: try to say that!). The arcade houses twenty stores that represent over 60 Greek publishing houses. Several of their books are exhibited in the display cases. Among the stores, you will notice a baby grand piano that is used for cultural events and a café where one can stop for a midday break.

Korais Square

Odos: At the University Metro Station

Across the street from the Neoclassical Triology, you will find Plateia Korais; you will recognize it immediately when you see the fountain that is encased with a glass pyramid in its center. The square is full of activity with Athenians patronizing the numerous stores, open-air cafés (including Starbucks) and a famous movie theater and health studio. There is even a Pizza Hut here - good place to stop for a bite. You will see that the Pizza Huts in Greece are much more elegant than those back home. And if you need to take a train somewhere, you can also enter/exit the Panepistimiou Metro Station at this point. Be sure to check out the works of Yianni Moralis, a very well known 20th century Greek visual artist, in the station before catching the train.

FOOTSTEPS THROUGH ATHINA

Yellow House • Residence of Soutsos-Rallis Family
Odos: 10 Koraes

Exactly opposite of the Neo-classical Greek Trilogy, you will notice a simple neoclassical building which stands out against the dark glass background of a modern building. Completed in 1842 or 1843, the house belonged to the Soutsos-Rallis family (political figures of the 20th century) and is one of the oldest buildings on Panepistimiou Street.

National Bank of Greece
Odos: 21 Panepistimiou (El. Venizelou)

The Bank of Greece was founded in 1928 but first situated down the street in the National Mortgage Bank. The present building, which has been listed as a historical monument, was inaugurated in 1938. Its structure truly represents the style that was used for interwar buildings.

Eleutheroudakis Bookstore
Odos: 17 Panepistimiou (El. Venizelou)
Hours: Monday - Friday: 9:00 am - 9:00 pm
Saturday: 9:00 am - 6:00 pm

Across the street from the Eye Clinic, you will notice a multi-story building built in marble and glass. This is Eleutheroudakis Bookstore - one of my favorite hangouts where I spend much time sorting through the large selection of Greek and English Books. It is the largest bookstore in Greece and there are several branches throughout Athens and the suburbs. The bookstore is comprised of eight floors and has a great children's department. If you get tired, take a break on the 6th floor café where you can choose from an array of drinks and snacks.

Attica Department Store

Odos: 9 Panepistimiou (El. Venizelou)
Hours: Mon-Fri.: 10:00am - 9:00pm
Saturday: 10:00am - 7:00pm

In 2005, the largest department store named Attica opened on Panepistimiou (El.Venizelou) Street in what was historically known as the Army Pension Fund building. During the German Occupation, this building was used as the Nazi headquarters. It is part of a multi-purpose complex that encompasses an entire block and is situated between two main boulevards: Panepistimiou (El. Venizelou) and Stadiou. In addition to the department store, the complex includes a health and fitness club, restaurants, the historically renovated theatres Pallas and Aliki, and Zonar Café; a coffeehouse that for years was frequented by all of the Athenian VIPs. Attica Department Store is huge; it has eight levels that comprises of 300 stores selling over 800 brand names for men, women and children. This is *definitely* the place to pick up gifts for those back home and to get something very European for you!

FOOTSTEPS THROUGH ATHINA

 HELPFUL GREEK WORDS

Η Οδός Βενιζέλου Ελευθερίου • Ee O<u>dos</u> Venee<u>ze</u>lou Elefthe<u>ree</u>ou • Venizelos Eleftherios Street

Η Οδός Πανεπιστημίου • Ee O<u>dos</u> Panepeestee<u>mee</u>ou • Panespistimiou Street

Το Νομισματικό Μουσείο Ηλίου Μέλαθρον • To Nomeesmatee<u>ko</u> Mou<u>see</u>o Ee<u>lee</u>ou <u>Me</u>lathron • Iliou Melathron Numismatic Museum

Ο ΄Αγιος Διονύσιος • O <u>A</u>yeeos Dee<u>o</u>nee<u>see</u>os • St. Dionysios

Ο Καθολικός Καθεδρικός • O Katholee<u>kos</u> Kathedree<u>kos</u> • The Catholic Cathedral

Η Οφθαλμολογική Κλινική • Ee Ofthamologee<u>kee</u> Kleenee<u>kee</u> • The Ophthalmology Eye Clinic

Η Ακαδημία Αθηνών • Ee Acadee<u>mee</u>a Athee<u>non</u> • The Academy of Athens

Το Πανεπιστημίο Αθηνών • To Panepeestee<u>mee</u>ou Athee<u>non</u> • The University of Athens

Η Εθνική Βιβλιοθήκη • Ee Etheenee<u>kee</u> Veevleo<u>thee</u>kee • The National Library

Το Θεατρικό Μουσείο • To Theatree<u>ko</u> Mou<u>see</u>o • The Theatre Museum

Το Αρσάκειο Μέγαρον • To Ar<u>sa</u>keeo <u>Me</u>garon • Arsakeio Building

Η Στοά του Βιβλίου • Ee Sto<u>a</u> tou Veev<u>lee</u>ou • Stoa tou Bibliou

Η Πλατεία Κοραή • Ee Pla<u>tee</u>a Ko<u>ra</u>yee • Korais Square

Το Κίτρινο Σπίτι-Η Οικία του Σούτσου Ράλλη • To <u>Kee</u>treeno <u>Spee</u>tee - Ee Ee<u>kee</u>a tou <u>Sout</u>sou <u>Ra</u>lee • The Yellow House -Residence of Soutsos-Rallis

Η Εθνική Τράπεζα της Ελλάδος • Ee Etheenee<u>kee</u> <u>Tra</u>peza tees El<u>la</u>dos • National Bank of Greece

Το Βιβλιοπωλείο Ελευθερουδάκης • To Veevleeopo<u>lee</u>o Eftheroudakees • Eleftheroudakis Bookstore

΄Αττικα Πολυκατάστημα • <u>A</u>teeka Poleeka<u>ta</u>steema • Attica Department Store

FOOTSTEPS THROUGH STADIOU STREET
KOLOKOTRONI SQUARE

Now let's walk over to the other main avenue that connects Omonia Square to Syntagma Square. It is called Stadiou Street. It can be reached by cutting through Korais Square; however, we are going to take a different route. Let's start by going south down Panepistimiou Street towards the end of Attica Department Store. Once we arrive at the corner (Panepistimiou and Voukouretsou), we will turn right and walk down towards the end of the block. We are now on Stadiou, a street with many department stores, jewelry stores and book arcades. Exactly across the street there is a rather small square surrounded by a few statues and a beautiful neoclassical building. It is called Kolokotroni Square, named after the Greek revolutionary war hero and commander in chief, Theodoros Kolokotronis, who was a *Klephtis* (rebel) leader that helped form a confederation of fighters in mainland Greece. He is highly remembered on March 25th - Greek Independence day - especially by Greek children who recite poems and sing songs in honor of him. You can't miss the huge, bronze equestrian statue of Kolokotronis in front of the square. It is an exact replica (1904) of a statue in Nafplion (in the eastern Argolid of the Peloponnese).

OLD PARLIAMENT HOUSE • NATIONAL HISTORICAL MUSEUM OF GREECE

Odos: 12 Stadiou
Hours: Tuesday - Sunday: 9:00a m - 2:00 pm

This is a prime example of neoclassical architecture and one of Greece's most historic buildings. Both the exterior and interior of the building are fabulous; be sure to check out the beautifully decorated ceiling in the Assembly Hall. The Old Parliament House (Palaia Vouli, in Greek) was built in 1871 and first served as the seat of the

National Assembly until it moved in 1932 to the current building that we already visited in Syntagma. Since 1961 it has served as the National Historical Museum of Greece. Sixteen rooms are dedicated to portraying Modern Greek history from the 15th century

AD to the present day. Among the many collections, you can find memorabilia from the Greek War of Independence, such as the bed and sword of the philhellene Lord Byron who fought and died for Greece's independence. The museum also has a great gift shop where you can find many gifts that represent Greece's unique history.

AGIOS GEORGIOS KARITSIS

Odos: Parnassou & Christou Lada

This three-aisled, domed basilica church is very near the Museum of the City of Athens. It was built in 1849 by Lysandros Kaftantzoglou, on the site of an older Byzantine Church that belonged to the Karykes family

(Karitsis). Lysandros maintained the Byzantine style and incorporated much of the material from the previous church into this one.

MUSEUM OF THE CITY OF ATHENS

Odos: 5 & 7 Paparrigopoulou
Hours: Monday-Wednesday-Thursday-Friday: 9:00 am - 4:00 pm
Saturday - Sunday: 10:00 am - 3:00 pm

As we walk through the square, you will notice another beautiful neoclassical building. It was the residence of Greece's first King

Footsteps Through Athina

Othon and Queen Amalia and is still often referred to as the Old Palace. There are actually two combined buildings that make up this edifice that today serves as the Museum of the City of Athens. Inaugurated in 1973, the museum presents the history of Athens from the middle-ages to the present day. In addition to the

strong emphasis on artifacts from the era of the Greek War of Independence, the museum features recreations of rooms from the Royal Palace, a typical Athenian living room from the 19th century and a small chapel. This is a fun place to visit and great for those of you who like stepping back into history.

Plateia Klafthmonas

Continuing down the street, we will approach a big square called Plateia Klafthmonas, which means "the square of the wailing", or grief. You might be wondering why and how a square took on such a strange name, so let me tell you the history behind it. During the 19th century, the houses around this square were rented to civil servants. Every time the government changed and the opposing party was elected, the previous civil servants were fired from their state jobs. They would gather around cafés in this square and cry of their fate and misfortune. The area around the square is known as the historical district and encompasses many governmental and municipal offices in addition to several banks, shops and restaurants. In 1989, a bronze statue (photo) of three, intertwined figures was erected in the square to celebrate 40 years of the end of the 1945-49 civil war. The statue is called the *National Reconciliation* and was designed by Vasilis Doropoulos.

Agioi Theodori

Odos: Dragatsaniou & Agion Theodori

The church of Agioi Theodori is located on the south-western side of Klafthmonas Square. On the western side of the church, you can find two marble plates with inscriptions mounted on the wall. The engraving on the one plate states that the church was renovated by Nikolaos Kalomolos, an administrative official of the Byzantine Empire. The second plate has an inscription of what appears to be look like "1065". Although there are many opposing opinions on what this date stands for, it is assumed that this church dates back to the 11th century based on its architectural and morphological characteristics that represent a church built in the middle Byzantine period. Some of these features are: the cross-in-square type; the church's windows and walls, which are arranged with bricks and stones; the three naves; and eight-sided dome. The adjoining bell tower is a more recent addition.

Panagia Chrissospiliotissa
Virgin Mary Chrissospliotissa

Odos: Aiolou & Chrissospilottissis

This church was built during the 19th century on the site of an older Byzantine church that was destroyed during the Greek War of Independence. Combining elements from various periods and styles of church building, the church is a two story building and quite impressive. There is a bell tower on each side of it.

FOOTSTEPS THROUGH ATHINA

AGIA PARASKEVI • ST. PARASKEVI

Odos: Aiolou & Athinas

This tiny, single-nave, barrel-vaulted church is very near to the Panagia Chrissospiliotissa. It was built during the Ottoman rule; however, the wall paintings were created much later. The church belongs to the Monastery of Phaneromeni.

 HELPFUL GREEK WORDS

Η Πλατεία Κολοκοτρώνη • Ee Plateea Kolokotronee • Kolokotroni Square

Το Μέγαρο της Παλαιάς Βουλής - Το Εθνικό Ιστορικό Μουσείο • To Megaro tees Paleas Voulees – To Etheneeko Eestoreeko Mouseeo • The Old Parliament House - National Historical Museum

Το Μουσείο της Πόλεως των Αθηνών • To Mouseeo tees Poleos ton Atheenon • The Museum of the City of Athens

Η Πλατεία Κλαυθμώνας • Ee Plateea Klafthmonas • Plateia Klafthmonas

Ο Άγιος Γεώργιος Καρύτσης • O Ayeeos Yeorgeeos Kareetsees • St. George Karitsis

Οι Άγιοι Θεόδωροι • Ee Ayee Theodoree • Saints Theodori

Η Παναγία Χρυσοσπηλίτισσα • Ee Panayeea Chreesospeeleeteesa • Panagia Virgin Mary Chrissospliotissa

Η Αγία Παρασκευή • Ee Ayeea Paraskevee • St. Paraskevi

FOOTSTEPS THROUGH OMONIA

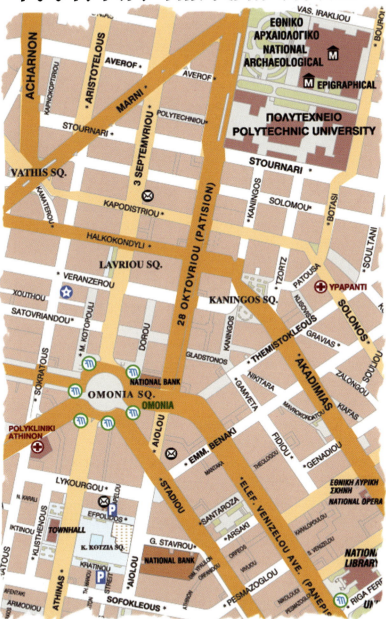

We will now visit Omonia Square and its surrounding neighborhood. It is the starting point for roads leading to different parts of the city and indeed one of the busiest sections of Athens. If we start out at Syntagma Square, two main boulevards (Panepistimiou and Stadiou) run directly into it. Before we venture off into the district around Omonia, let's learn a bit about the history of this square.

Omonia Square (the Square of Concord-Unity) is the oldest square in the city and considered to be the commercial heart of Modern Athens. It is always full of a lot of traffic and noise as it is bound with several offices, renovated hotels, department stores,  shops, traditional old Greek coffee shops and one of the main Metro stations. In the center of the square you will see a fountain (erected in the 1950's) and gardens. The square was designed in the 19th century under the renowned architects Kleanthis and Schaubert. It was originally intended to be the site of the royal palace, which we visited in Syntagma Square, and was to be named after King Otto, with his statue displayed. However, after the ousting of the monarchy in 1862, the area became populist, and this is why it took the name Omonia - which stands for unity.

As the city grew, the square became circular, connecting some of the busiest commercial streets (Pireos, Panepistimiou, Stadiou, Athinas, Agiou Konstandinou, 3 Septemvriou, Patission) and it became a major city hub with neoclassical buildings emerging throughout the neighborhood. Unfortunately, throughout the late 20th century, Omonia Square deteriorated and became a seedy hangout. With the renovation of the city in preparation for the Athens Olympics 2004, the square received a facelift and it is once again a thriving beautiful *plateia*.

OMONIA METRO STATION

Another fascinating Athenian Metro Station! Omonia's train station actually has a very long history. In 1895, the first subway station opened in Omonia beneath Athenas Street near the central market. At this time, trains were steam operated and remained like this until ten years later when they were replaced with electrically operated ones.

As the city grew and traffic increased, the need for a new station arose. In 1930 the present underground station at Omonia was inaugurated. The new station provided three platforms and two tracks allowing trains to open on both sides. Throughout the 20th century, additional stations opened and it was then possible to travel north via Omonia Station. In 1957, the Line 1 train ran from Piraeus to Kifissia. In the late 1990's, reconstruction began on the Athens Metro System and Omonia Station underwent many changes. The main goal was not only to modernize it; but to retain many of the original features of the station. In 2000, the newly renovated Omonia Metro Station opened with a new line and an additional underground platform - making it an interchange station.

Today, this efficient Metro station is state-of-the-art and, as are so many other Metro stations in Athens, Omonia is a museum filled with pieces of antiquity and artwork. When you go downstairs, you can see old photos of what Omonia was like during the 19th and early 20th centuries. In the first transfer level area, you can take a look at the superb work of the contemporary artist Nikos Kessanlis entitled "Queue" which portrays scenes of people strolling through the station. On another transfer level is Pavlos' "Football" - six banners covered with confetti that the public helped decorate. Traveling by train in Athens is both enjoyable and educational.

Kotzia and City Hall Squares

If we walk south down Athinas Street (one of the major connecting streets of Omonia) we will soon reach Kotzia Square. Although it is considered to be one of the most impressive and vibrant Athenian squares today (thanks to the Athens 2004 renovation plan), for a number of years it was in a state of total devastation. Kotzia Square was named after a former mayor of Athens, Constantinos Kotzias, who served during the dictatorship of Ioannis Metaxas (during the 1930's). The square is also called National Resistance Square (Ethnikis Antistaseos) in reference to the struggle against the German Occupation. It is also called City Hall Square (Dimarcheio) - for you will find the City Hall of Athens. Near the City Hall you will notice a

fountain with geysers and a huge, curvilinear statue called "Theseus" that was designed and donated by the Greek sculptor, Sophia Bari. There are a number of interesting buildings and sites to see here; let's go visit them!

Archaeological Site in Kotzia Square

In addition to viewing both neoclassical and modern buildings in Kotzia Square, you can also see a remarkable archaeological site opposite the Athens City Hall. The excavations were first discovered in 1985-1988 during the construction of an underground parking lot, and continuously during the next two decades (especially during the Unification of Athens Project). The archaeological findings consist of three ancient streets; a wall; a cemetery filled with many important objects dating back to the Protogeometric period (9th century BC) and up to the Late Roman period (3rd century AD); pottery workshops from the Late Roman period (late 3rd-4th century AD); and several houses. The findings have provided information and evidence about the fortification of Ancient Athens. They have also shown that an ancient road began at the Archarnian Gate and led to the northern districts of Attica. A number of these findings are showcased under glass covers.

Melas Mansion · National Bank of Greece

Odos: 86 Aiolou

On the southeastern side of the square, you will find the former Melas Mansion. It was designed by the famous Ernst Miller in 1883 and first served as a place to accommodate wealthy Greeks from abroad when they visited Athens, and then as the Central Post Office of Athens. It now houses art exhibitions and offices of the National Bank of Greece. Next door, the National Bank of Greece has its administrative offices in a new, grand building. While here, be sure to check out the archaeological finds that were recently discovered during the Unification of Athens, which are just to the right of the building.

Athens City Hall

Odos: Athinas - Plateia Kotzia
Hours: Monday – Friday: 8:30 am - 3:00 pm

On the west side of the plateia you will find a beautiful neoclassical building which serves as the *Dimarcheio* (people's home), or Athens City Hall. Built and inaugurated in 1874, the City Hall started out as a one-story building (in Europe, this means that there are two floors:

the ground floor and the floor above it). In 1901, Mayor Spyros Mercouris (Melina Mercouri's grandfather) demanded that the building be renovated. In 1935-36 (under Mayor Kotzias), another floor was added that included beautiful painted frescoes with motifs highlighting the history of Athens from antiquity to modern times. In 1983, City Hall moved to a new location; however, in 1987, after realizing the importance of this building, it returned to the original site. The building is stunning both inside and out and very much worth visiting. Upon entering it, you will see bronze busts of Pericles - the great statesman and important leader during the Golden Age of Athens - and Aspasia, Pericles' influential wife. You can then ascend the magnificent, red carpeted marble staircase leading up to the Mayor's office and gaze at the magnificent stained-glassed windows that depict Athens in myth and history.

ATHENS CENTRAL MARKET • VARVAKIOS
Odos: 42 Athinas
Hours: Monday - Saturday: 8:00 am - 6:00 pm

Across the street from Kotzia Square you will find the Athens Central Market; a concept that originated in Ancient Athens and is still so alive today. For many centuries, vendors would sell their produce around the ancient Agora and, in 1875, Mayor Panagis Kyriakos decided to build a modern day market. Ten years later, the glass roofed, neoclassical building with high archways opened to the public. What a fun place to visit and familiarize yourself with so many products that make up the Greek cuisine. You can realistically spend hours here shopping or just looking at the

great selections of fruit, vegetables, meat, seafood, herbs, spices, cheeses and sweets from all over Greece. And do note that the prices are much lower here than in supermarkets - and everything is so fresh! You can even eat at one of the four neighboring restaurants that make use of the market's specialties. The market has many halls of produce stands. Meat is sold in an adjacent  building that is attached by walkways. Check out the way that the butchers display their products - much different than back home. A word of caution: the fish market's floor is often wet and can be quite slippery, so be careful to wear the appropriate shoes!

NATIONAL TECHNICAL UNIVERSITY OF ATHENS POLYTECHNION

Odos: 28 Oktovriou

Now, from the Central Market on Athinas Street, we can walk east over to the next parallel street, Aiolou. Let's turn left (north) here and take this back towards Omonia Square. At  this point the street is called 28 Oktovriou Street (Patision). We will continue here for about eight blocks and eventually arrive at the National Technical University of Athens, or Polytechnion, as most Greeks call it.

This is one of the most prestigious universities in Greece. It was founded as the Royal School of Arts in 1836 shortly after Greece gained independence, offering part time classes on Saturdays and public holidays. Four years later, it became a daily technical school and was housed in a building on Pireos Street. In 1843, the institution was renamed the School of Arts and the School of Industrial Arts, offering more classes and departments. It rapidly grew into a technical university and in 1873 moved to Patision Street. It was once again renamed, this time as the Ethnic Metsovion Polytechnic in honor of its benefactors whose origin was from the town of Metsovo in Epirus. The original neoclassical building complex was designed by Lysandros Kaftantzoglou and consisted of three buildings. Eventually, more buildings were added for the expanding departments and schools. Today the university is divided into nine academic faculties offering several degrees in engineering, architecture, mathematics and physics.

The Polytechnion has always had a vibrant political life and has contributed greatly to Modern Greek history. It is remembered for the student uprising against the colonel's dictatorship of November 17, 1973 that escalated to an open antijunta revolt. Unfortunately, this event ended in bloodshed with many students loosing their lives. Every year demonstrations and memorials take place in commemoration of those students. Wreaths are placed on a university monument that is inscribed with the names of the Polytechnic students that were killed. Greek schools and universities remain closed on this very solemn day.

NATIONAL ARCHAEOLOGICAL MUSEUM
Odos: 44 Patission
Hours: Monday: 1:00 pm - 7:30 pm
Tuesday - Sunday: 8:00 am - 7:30 pm

Our next stop is the National Archaeological Museum, which is next door to the Polytechnio. Inaugurated in 1881, the museum is housed in a beautiful, 19th century neoclassical building that was designed by L. Lange and remodeled by Ernst Ziller. In 2004, the museum closed for about eight months for renovations. It is now completely air conditioned and in excellent condition.

Footsteps Through Athina

This is the largest museum in Greece. It has several galleries on two floors that display more than 20,000 exhibits of treasures and collections from all over Greece, ranging from Prehistory to Late Antiquity. The museum houses six permanent collections: The Prehistoric Collection, with works from the Neolithic, Cycladic, Mycenaean Civilization and from the settlement of Thera; The Sculptures Collection - 7th to 15th century BC; The Vase and Minor Objects Collection - 11th century BC to the Roman Period; The Stathatos Collection, with objects from all periods; The Metallurgy Collection - statues, figurines and objects; and The Egyptian and Near Eastern Antiquities Collection - pre-dynastic period (5000 BC) to the Roman conquest.

There are so many notable archaeological treasures to see here and you really need a lot of time to spend in this museum. Among my favorites are: the gold funerary mask (often called the Mask of Agamemnon), discovered by Schliemann, among other finds from the vaulted tombs in Mycenae; the statue of Diadoumenos; the Cycladic Harp player; the famous bronze Poseidon Statue from Cape Artemsion; the horse and jockey statue from Artemsion; the Boy from Marathon bronze statue; the Kouros Statues; wall paintings from Tiryns; and a statue of Hermes.

Be sure to pick up a brochure at the entrance; it is quite detailed and will help you find all of the exhibits as you go around the museum. Also while there, be sure to visit the gift store for some exclusive gifts and apparel.

FOOTSTEPS THROUGH ATHINA

EPIGRAPHICAL MUSEUM
NATIONAL ARCHAEOLOGICAL MUSEUM

Odos: 1 Tositsa
Hours: Tuesday - Sunday: 8:30 am - 3:00 pm

While at the National Archaeological Museum, be sure to stop by the  Epigraphical Museum that is housed in the south wing of the ground floor of the museum. Founded in 1885, it is the largest of its kind in the world. It contains over 13,510 Greek inscriptions from Attica and other districts of Greece. In ancient Greece, important documents were chiseled into marble stones. The inscriptions record resolutions, laws, letters, tax lists and financial accounts. The purpose of this museum is to safeguard, protect, and display the collections of such important epigraphs.

HELPFUL GREEK WORDS

Η Πλατεία Ομονοίας • Ee Plateea Omoneeas • Plateia Omonia

Ο Σταθμός Μετρό Ομονοίας • O Sthathmos Metro Omoneeas • Omonia Metro Station

Η Πλατεία Κοτζιά-Η Πλατεία Δημαρχείου • Ee Plateea Kotzeea-Ee Plateea Deemarheeou • Kotzia Square - City Hall Square

Τα Αρχαιολογικά Ευρήματα στην Πλατεία Κοτζιά • Ta Archeologeeka Evreemata steen Plateea Kotzia • The Archaeological findings in Kotzia Square

Το Μέγαρο Μελάς- Η Εθνική Τράπεζα της Ελλάδος • To Megaro Melas - Ee Ethneekee Trapeza tees Elados • Melas Mansion - National Bank of Greece

Το δημαρχείο • To Deemarheeo • City Hall

Η Κεντρική Αγορά της Αθήνας Βαρβάκειος • Ee Kentreekee Agora tees Atheenas Varvakeeos • Athens Central Market Varvakios

Το Πολυτεχνείο • To Poleetechneeo • The Polytechnion

Το Επιγραφικό Μουσείο • To Epeegrafeeko Mouseeo • The Epigraphical Museum

FOOTSTEPS THROUGH THE OUTSKIRTS OF ATHENS

Most visitors to Greece spend the majority of their time visiting all the sites and treasures around the center of Athens. While there is so much to see in this metropolis, it is well worth your time to venture out into the neighboring suburbs and discover the uniqueness and beauty that is often missing from the visitor's itinerary. So, come with me as I introduce you to some of my favorite suburbs (please note that this is only a small portion of the suburbs that exist in each section).

THE NORTHERN SUBURBS

Aghia Paraskevi, Drosia, Ekali, Filothei, Halandri, Kefalari, Kifissia, Maroussi, Melissia, Pendeli, Psychiko and Vrilissia.

The northern suburbs are the areas on the southwest slopes of Penteli Mountain. Due to the elevation, several of these suburbs are much cooler than in the center of Athens. They can be accessed via Kiffisias Avenue and a number of them can be reached by the Metro. The bus will get you to all of them.

The northern suburbs are quite affluent districts where you will find many beautiful villas surrounded by lush gardens. In fact, the suburb of Ekali is the 3rd richest area of Europe. The aristocratic suburb of Kifissia is home to many political families. It also is a very recreational neighborhood for all ages because of its many shops, movie theaters, restaurants and nightclubs. The Goulandris Museum of Natural History (13 Levidou St) is located here displaying a wealth of exhibits. It is both a museum and a research center for the Greek flora, fauna, geology, and paleontology. (Hours: Weekdays: 9:00 am - 2:30 pm & Sundays: 10:00 am - 2:30 pm)

The suburbs of Kifissia, Halandri, Aghia Paraskevi and Maroussi (home to the Athens 2004 Olympic Stadium) boast great boutiques, shops and malls. Aghia Paraskevi takes pride in its several great pizzerias, bars and restaurants that are located around Aghia Paraskevi Square, where you can also find its lovely cathedral.

The Southern Suburbs

Alimos, Glyfada, Palaio Faliro, Vari, Varkiza, Voula and Vouliagmeni

Athens is one of the few cities in the world where you can quickly reach the beach resorts from the center of town. Located along the Apollo Coast, or Athenian Riviera as it is often called, these elegant suburbs host a number of sandy beaches, beautiful homes, shopping centers and restaurants. For more information on the beaches in this area, check out the Sports and Leisure chapter.

The Eastern Suburbs

Cholargos, Papagou, Vyronas and Zografou

These suburbs are surrounded by the Ymittos Mountain range and are primarily inhabited by middle and upper income groups. Nestled between urbanized residential areas and business complexes, the neighborhoods have become home to several new shopping, eating and recreational centers. Zografou is home to Panepistimiopoulos, the campus of the University of Athens, and is filled with many services and recreation for all.

THE WESTERN SUBURBS

Egaleo, Ilion, Nikaia, Peristeri and Petroupoli

The western suburbs are resided primarily by middle to low income groups. Peristeri is home to a large number of foreign immigrants. It has a large industrial area that has recently been modernized and transformed into a lively new entertainment spot.

HELPFUL GREEK WORDS

Τα βόρεια Προάστια • Τα Voreea Proasteea • The Northern Suburbs
Τα Νότια Προάστια • Τα Noteea Proasteea • The Southern Suburbs
Τα Ανατολικά Προάστια • Τα Anatoleeka Proasteea • The Eastern Suburbs
Τα Δυτικά Προάστια • Τα Deeteeka Proasteea • The Western Suburbs

CAPE SOUNION

Cape Sounion, one of the most visited and picturesque sites in Greece, is located at the southern-most tip of the Attica peninsula. It is renowned for the ruins of the ancient Temple of Poseidon, the mythological god of the sea. Perched high on a dramatic cliff, the Temple of Poseidon overlooks the blue Aegean Sea and islands. The view is magnificent, with sunset the most popular time to be there.

The temple was built during the 5th century BC on the site of an older temple that was destroyed by the Persians. It is believed that the Temple of Poseidon was designed by the same architect that designed the Temple of Hephaestos in the Ancient Agora. Although the Temple of Poseidon only retains 16 Doric order columns from the original edifice, it is easily understood how magnificent this temple once was. At one time, the temple housed a large statue of Poseidon in its main hall. All that remains today of the statue is a foot which is stored in the Poros Museum. On a lower hill near the Temple of Poseidon lies the Sanctuary of Athena with two temples dedicated to the goddess.

In ancient times, the Temple of Poseidon served as a landmark for mariners. Upon seeing the white columns, they knew that they were close to Piraeus. Legend has it that King Aegeus of Athens leaped to his death at Cape Sounion when he saw a ship returning from Crete with a black sail on it, thinking that it symbolized that his son had died in battle with the Minotaur. Unfortunately, he was wrong; his son was still alive!

So inspired by this awesome site was Lord Byron on his visit to the temple in 1810, that he inscribed his name on one of the columns. Try to find it on your visit to the site. The Temple of Poseidon is open every day of the year. Within walking distance, there is also a hotel and a taverna where you can stop and have some ice cream, a dessert or something to drink.

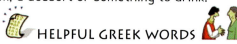

HELPFUL GREEK WORDS

Το Σούνιο • To Souneeo • Sounio
Ο Ναός του Ποσειδώνα • O Naos tou Poseedona • Temple of Poseidon

PIRAEUS

Piraeus is the third largest city in Greece - in terms of population - and serves as its main seaport. Today it is the largest port in Europe and the third largest in the world in terms of passenger transportation, transporting 19,000,000 passengers annually. It currently serves only passenger boats, as commercial cargo ship ports have been moved to different areas. After the 2004 Olympic Games, the port

underwent modernization and it is now one of the most beautiful harbors in the Mediterranean.

Piraeus has been the port of Athens for more than 2,500 years. In medieval times, it was known as Porto Leone. A huge marble lion, that once guarded the port's entrance, was stolen in 1688 during the invasion by Francesco Morozini and brought to Venice, Italy, where it still stands today. A copy of this lion can be viewed at the Piraeus Archaeological Museum.

Throughout the past century, Piraeus has inspired many famous writers, composers and singers such as Theodorakis, Xarhakos and Hadjidakis, and film makers such as Jules Dassin. This is the place where Melina Mercouri filmed *Never on Sunday*. Several songs have been dedicated to Piraeus, most probably because it embraces a very sentimental and nostalgic setting for many; the place where many Greeks said their last goodbyes. It is from this port where seamen used to leave for years of traveling the sea and it is also from this port where thousands of Greek immigrants departed for a new life in other countries.

In addition to the main port, Piraeus boasts two other lovely ancient ones; the Zea harbor and Munichia. Zea, known today as Pasalimani, is one of the largest marinas in the Mediterranean. You will see many attractive yachts along the harbor, in addition to a number of great restaurants. A bit west of Pasalimini is the neighborhood of Peiraiki, the best place for fresh fish and seafood with a gorgeous view of the Saronic Gulf, Salamis and Aegina. There is also a Nautical Museum located here, comprised of nine rooms that display the naval history of Greece from prehistoric times to present (Odos: Akti Themistokleous & Freattys).

Munichia, also known as Mikrolimano or Tourkolimano, is the second yacht marina of the port and very picturesque. Many tourists enjoy eating at the local fish tavernas and restaurants that are surrounded by dazzling yachts and fishing boats. The panoramic hill of Kastelia is directly above. It is a great spot to see traditional Greek homes and you can't beat the view - bring your camera!

There are a number of noteworthy sites to see in the city center of Piraeus. Let's take a look:

Piraeus Metro Station: The neoclassical building is stunning and definitely a station that brings you back into time. Line 1 (Green Line) from Monasteraki will get you here.

St. Spiridonas Church: The oldest and most historic church in town.

Cathedral of the Holy Trinity: A red church with an incredible dome.

Archaeological Museum of Piraeus: (31 Charilaou Trikoupi) The first museum was built in 1935 and an extension was added on in 1966. It houses very fine collections of funerary reliefs dating back from the 5th & 4th centuries BC, pottery from excavations in the area, Hellenistic and Roman Sculpture from Piraeus and much more.

Municipal Theatre at Korai Square: Another magnificent neoclassical building!

Municipal Gallery of Piraeus: (91 Iroon Polytechniou) Inaugurated in 1957, this gallery began to operate as a section of the Municipal Library. In 1985 it became independent and today houses 837 fabulous works by notable Greek artists, including the extensive collection of modern sculpture by Georgios Kastriotis and theatrical memorabilia donated by Manos Katrakis.

Shopping Area: The main shopping section of Piraeus is located on Gounari Street. In addition to great clothing stores, you will find several shops selling exotic herbs and spices.

A short distance away is Neo Phaliro where the Stadium of Peace & Friendship is located. This stadium hosts athletic events, concerts and exhibitions. The impressive Karaiskakis Stadium is an indoor arena and home to Olympiakos basketball and football.

HELPFUL GREEK WORDS
Ο Πειραιάς • O Peerayas • Piraeus

FOOTSTEPS THROUGH ATHINA

SPECIAL EVENTS
2004 ATHENS OLYMPICS

"Unforgettable Dream Games"; - these were the words of the International Olympic Committee president, Jacques Rogge, in his speech at the Closing Ceremonies of the Athens 2004 Olympics. These games had a special importance in my life as I was very fortunate to be an official Olympic volunteer/translator for 17 glorious days. It was such a wonderful experience and so important that I include it in this book, as the Athens Olympics recreated and gave a new image to the beautiful city that you have been introduced to through these chapters.

The years, months and days leading up to the Olympics were met with much criticism and doubts that Athens would be ready for the event due to construction delays, security threats and serious cost issues. While the world feared that Athens just wouldn't pull it off, Mayor Dora Bakogianni reassured all saying that "We are Greeks doing the *Syrtaki*", a Greek dance that starts off slow and rapidly progresses in the end. And this is exactly what happened; not only was Athens ready, but it proved that it was capable of presenting the very best Olympics ever! From the highest tech venues to ceremonies that portrayed both its glorious historical and cultural past, along with the new modern face of today's city, Athens truly shined as the Olympic Games returned back home to their origin! So now come with me as our footsteps return to the magical moments of this spectacular Olympic homecoming.

GENERAL FACTS ABOUT THE GAMES

The Olympic Games were held from August 13-29, 2004. 28 sports were represented in 37 extraordinary Olympic venues that extended through various neighborhoods and suburbs of Athens. All of the events were very accessible by the new Metro system, tram and other means of transportation.

10,625 athletes competed from 202 countries. In fact, this was the first time since the 1996 Summer Olympics that all countries with a National Olympic Committee were in attendance. There were 301 medal events. The award ceremonies were truly authentic and quite moving. The Athens Olympics revived an ancient practice stemming back to Greek antiquity by adorning its three medal winners with a *kotinos*, a crown made from olive leaves.

The Olympic Emblem

The emblem for the Athens 2004 Olympic Games was the Kotinos, a branch from an olive tree intertwined into a circle. It originates from Ancient Greece and was the official honorary award of the Olympic Champions. The olive tree was also the sacred tree of Athens. It therefore represents the city of Athens where democracy and civilization was founded. The white and blue colors of the emblem symbolize the colors of the Greek flag.

Olympic Torch and Relay

The Athens 2004 Olympic torch that carried the official Olympic flame was designed to resemble an olive leaf. The lighting ceremony of the torch took place on March 25 (Greek Independence Day) in Ancient Olympia and then traveled around the entire world. The theme for this event was "Our Flame Unites the World" and this is exactly what happened. The 2004 Olympic Torch Relay brought the Olympic flame to five continents around the world in 65 days. It was the first time that the flame traveled to Africa, India and South America. The flame arrived at both former Olympic cities and other large cities before returning to Greece. In the Opening Ceremony of the Olympic Games in Athens (August 13, 2004), the torch lit the flame in the OAKA Olympic Stadium. It remained lit until the Closing Ceremony. It was so awe-inspiring walking around the stadium illuminated by this flame.

Olympic Mascots

Since the 1968 Winter Olympics in Grenoble France, it has been an Olympic tradition to have a mascot for the games. The Athens 2004 Olympics had two official mascots; a sister Athina and brother Phevos (pronounced Fivos in Greek). They were named after Athena, the goddess of wisdom, strategy and war, and Phoebos, the god of light and music. They were modeled after ancient terra cotta *daidala*, dolls from the 7th century BC that can be viewed in the National Archaeological Museum in Athens. Although their creation and names are linked to ancient Greece, the two children represented the link between Greek history and the modern Olympic Games. Their image was seen all over the country during the Olympic Games on clothing, pins and other Olympic memorabilia. The mascots also visited the venues and sites around Athens, bringing pleasure and smiles to all!

OAKA · Athens Olympic Sports Complex

The Olympic Sports Complex - OAKA in Maroussi (a northern suburb in Athens) was the major stadium that hosted the 2004 Olympic Games. It was also here where the Opening and Closing Ceremonies took place. The stadium is also referred to as the Spiros Louis Stadium. He was the winner of the Marathon at the first, modern day 1896 Summer Olympics in Athens and is considered a national hero.

The stadium was originally designed in 1979 and since then it has hosted a number of events. It went through major renovation for the Olympics, and this state-of-the-art stadium is best known for the architectural creativity of the famous Spanish architect Santiago Calatrava. The complex includes monuments, gardens and futuristic passages. The stadium has two huge arches that support a massive, steel and blue glass roof above the enormous stands. The Olympic Complex also comprises an indoor basketball hall, the aquatic center, the Olympic tennis center and the velodrome.

Olympic Volunteers

Much of the success of the Athens 2004 Olympic Games is owed to the 45,000 volunteers who supported every athlete, spectator and visitor at this event and charmed all with their kindness and dedication. These volunteers were of all ages, cultures and backgrounds and came from 188 countries. They all had one thing in common: they shared the passion for the Olympic Ideal and Olympism. I am so honored that I was one of them!

Although the games lasted for only 17 days, it entailed many more for the volunteers. The work was very strenuous and volunteers devoted many days to training, tours and accreditation checks. Feet were sore as we stood for hours with temperature soaring over 100 degrees. We worked 10 hour shifts, usually leaving the stadium at 1:30 in the morning and often starting work as early as 4:00 a.m. We helped seat guests, tore ticket stubs and even helped security search for bombs. Although we were often exhausted, we never stopped smiling nor did we cease to show what Greek hospitality was all about. In the end, we were told that *we* had won the gold medal.

You could immediately spot the volunteers; they were everywhere in their colorful Adidas uniforms and big badges. I will never forget the moment I received my official uniform. I couldn't wait to wear it; and when I did put it on, I was so proud walking around the city, for I officially represented Greece and the Athens 2004 Olympics. In addition to the satisfaction that we gained for volunteering, we also developed friendships with volunteers from all over the world and new bonds were created that are still intact. It was indeed an honor being a volunteer and a lifelong experience that I am so happy to have had.

THE OPENING CEREMONY

The Opening Ceremony (August 13, 2004) of the Athens 2004 Olympics was praised throughout world as being the best opening ceremony in history. Anyone who was present at this magnificent event can testify that it was extraordinary! The magical ceremony, brilliantly created, designed and directed by Dimitris Papaioannou, elaborated on the traditional Greek culture from its mythological beginnings through the progression of Greek art. Dramatic Greek traditional music combined by the beat of a drummer accompanied a performance that portrayed over 3,000 years of Greece's enormous historical past. From archaic statues to elaborate, colorful costumes and never before seen technologies, the performance captivated spectators throughout the world, showing all the country that gave birth to democracy, philosophy, theater, sports and the Olympic Games!

FOOTSTEPS THROUGH ATHINA

THE CLOSING CEREMONY

The Closing Ceremony of the Athens Olympics took place on August 29, 2004. The stadium was transformed into a huge wheat field amid traditional Greek music and dancing. Replacing the historical context of the Opening Ceremony, this festive event highlighted the Greeks' pride in their culture and country and centered on Greek folk and pop themes with a variety of musical performances by several of Greece's singers. Mayor Bakoyianni passed the Olympic flag to the Beijing (the next to host the Olympics in 2008) mayor. This was followed by a cultural performance and glimpse into Chinese culture. Short speeches were given by Gianna Angelopoulos-Daskalaki, chief organizer of the Games, and by Jacques Rogge, the International Olympic Committee president. In his speech, Rogge praised and thanked Athens for the unforgettable dream games. The Olympic flame was then extinguished marking an end to the fabulous Athens 2004 Olympics. And as you can imagine, a giant party followed the ceremony. *Opa!* Greeks sure know how to celebrate!

 HELPFUL GREEK WORDS

Οι Ολυμπιακοί Αγώνες Αθήνα 2004 • Ee Oleembeea<u>kee</u> A<u>go</u>nes A<u>thee</u>na 2004 • The Olympic Games Athens 2004

Ο Κότινος • O Ko<u>tee</u>nos • The Kotinos - Crown

Η Ολυμπιακή Φλόγα • Ee Oleembea<u>kee</u> <u>Flo</u>ga • The Olympic Flame

Η Αθηνά και ο Φοίβος • Ee A<u>thee</u>na ke o <u>Fee</u>vos • Athena & Phevos

ΟΑΚΑ - Το Ολυμπιακό Αθλητικό Κέντρο Αθηνών • OAKA - To Oleempeeia<u>ko</u> Athlee<u>ti</u>ko <u>Ken</u>tro Athee<u>non</u> • OAKA - The Olympic Athletic Center of Athens

Οι Εθελοντές • Ee Ethe<u>lon</u>tes • The Volunteers

Η Τελετή Έναρξης • Ee Tele<u>tee</u> E<u>nar</u>ksees • The Opening Ceremony

Η Τελετή Λήξης • Ee Tele<u>tee</u> <u>Lee</u>ksees • The Closing Ceremony

GREEK LANGUAGE AND EDUCATION

The Greek Alphabet consists of 24 letters. Surprisingly, half of these letters appear exactly the same in the English alphabet, so if you can learn the other half, you should have no problem reading signs and menus in Greek.

GREEK ALPHABET

Capital Letter	Lower Case	Name of Letter	Pronunciation
Α	α	άλφα	alpha
Β	β	Βήτα	veeta
Γ	γ	γάμμα	gama
Δ	δ	δέλτα	thelta
Ε	ε	έψιλον	epseelon
Ζ	ζ	ζήτα	zeta
Η	η	ήτα	eeta
Θ	θ	θήτα	theta
Ι	ι	ιώτα	yota
Κ	κ	κάππα	kapa
Λ	λ	λάμβδα	lamtha
Μ	μ	μι	mee
Ν	ν	νι	nee
Ξ	ξ	ξι	ksee
Ο	ο	όμικρον	omeekron
Π	π	πι	pee
Ρ	ρ	ρο	ro
Σ	σ ς	σίγμα	seegma
Τ	τ	ταυ	taf
Υ	υ	ύψιλον	eepseelon
Φ	φ	φι	fee
Χ	χ	χι	hee
Ψ	ψ	ψι	psee
Ω	ω	ωμέγα	omega

FOOTSTEPS THROUGH ATHINA

THE GREEK CONSONANTS
β,γ,δ,ζ,θ,κ,λ,μ,ν,ξ,π,ρ,σ,τ,φ,χ,ψ

THE GREEK VOWELS
α,ε,η,ι,ο,υ,ω

COMBINATION OF VOWELS OR CONSONANTS

The Greek language often combines two vowels (diphthongs) or two consonants (diagraphs) together to make up one sound. They are as follows:

GREEK VOWEL COMBINATIONS

ου sounds like the English 'oo' in zoo
αι sounds like the English 'e' in get
αυ sounds like the English 'av' (as in 'average') or 'af' in after
ευ sounds like the English 'ev' (as in 'every") or 'ef in left
ει οι υι all three sound like the English 'ee' in beet

GREEK CONSONANT COMBINATIONS

μπ b as is bed
ντ d as is dog
γκ g as in gift
γγ ng as is angel
τσ ts as in cats
τζ dz as in dads

THE ESSENTIAL BASICS

Hello	Γεία σας	Ya sas
	Χαίρετε	He<u>re</u>te
Goodbye	Αντίο	A<u>dee</u>o
Good morning	Καλημέρα	Kalee<u>me</u>ra
Good evening	Καλησπέρα	Kalee<u>spe</u>ra
Good night	Καληνύχτα	Kale<u>nee</u>kta
Please	Παρακαλώ	Parakal<u>o</u>

FOOTSTEPS THROUGH ATHINA

Thank you	Ευχαριστώ πολύ	Efha<u>ree</u>sto po<u>lee</u>
Yes	Ναι, Μάλιστα	Ne, m<u>a</u>leesta
No	Όχι	<u>O</u>hee
Sorry/Excuse me	Συγγνώμη	Seeg<u>no</u>mee
Good	Καλό	Ka<u>lo</u>
Bad	Κακό	Ka<u>ko</u>
Beautiful	Ωραίο	Or<u>e</u>o
Okay	Εντάξει	En<u>da</u>ksee
Never mind	Δεν πειράζει	Then pee<u>ra</u>zee

HELPFUL EXPRESSIONS

How are you? Singular	Τι κάνεις;	Tee k<u>a</u>nees?
Plural or Polite	Τι κάνετε;	Tee k<u>a</u>nete?
Very well, thank you	Πολύ καλά ευχαριστώ	Po<u>lee</u> ka<u>la</u> efha<u>ree</u>sto
Do you speak Greek?		
Singular	Μιλάς Ελληνικά;	Mee<u>las</u> elleenee<u>ka</u>?
Plural or Polite	Μιλάτε Ελληνικά	Mee<u>late</u> elleenee<u>ka</u>?
I speak a little.	Μιλάω λίγο.	Mee<u>lao</u> <u>lee</u>go
I understand.	Καταλαβαίνω.	Katala<u>ve</u>no
I don't understand.	Δεν καταλαβαίνω	Then katala<u>ve</u>no.
What is your name?		
Singular	Πως σε λένε;	Pos se <u>le</u>ne?
Plural or Polite	Πως σας λένε;	Pos sas <u>le</u>ne?
My name is	Με λένε	Me <u>le</u>ne
Where is	Που είναι	Poo <u>ee</u>ne
Right	δεξιά	deks<u>eea</u>
Left	αριστερά	areeste<u>ra</u>
When?	Πότε;	<u>Po</u>te?
How much does it cost?	Πόσο κάνει;	<u>Po</u>so k<u>a</u>nee?
How much do they cost?	Πόσο κάνουν;	<u>Po</u>so k<u>a</u>noon?
Why?	Γιατί;	Yia<u>tee</u>?
What is this?	Τι είναι αυτό;	Tee <u>ee</u>ne af<u>to</u>?
I want	θέλω	<u>The</u>lo

Footsteps Through Athina

Greek Meals & Appetizers

English	Greek	Pronunciation
Beef	βοδινό	votheeno
Chicken	κοτόπουλο	kotopoolo

Dolmades • Vine leaves stuffed with meat, onions and rice
ντολμάδες — dolmathes

| Egg | αυγό | avgo |
| Fish | ψάρι | psari |

Gyros • Sliced pork/beef and served with a special white cucumber and yogurt sauce. It can be served on a pita bread or on the skewer.
γύρος — yeeros

Hamburger (Greek)	μπιφτέκι	beeftekee
Kalamaraki Fried squid	καλαμαράκια	kalamarakeea
Keftadakia-Meatballs	κεφτεδάκια	keftedakeea
Lamb	αρνί	arnee
Octopus	οχταπόδια	oktopodeea
Meat	κρέας	kreas

Mousakas • Layers of eggplant and minced meat topped with béchamel sauce
μουσακάς — moosakas

Pastitchio • Greek Style Lasagna
παστίτσιο — pastitsio

Pita (bread)	πίτα	peeta
Pork	χοιρινό	heereeno
Sausage	λουκάνικο	lookaneeko
Soup avgolemeno	σούπα αυγολέμενο	soupa avgolemeno
Souvlaki-shish kebab	σουβλάκι	souvlakee

Spanikopita • Phyllo pastry pie filled with spinach and feta cheese.
σπανακόπιτα — spanakopeeta

| Stuffed tomatoes | γεμιστά ντομάτες | yemeesta domates |

Tiropita • Phyllo pastry pie filled with feta cheese
τυρόπιτα — teeropeeta

Sauces & Side Dishes

Bread	ψωμί	ps**o**mee
Butter	βούτερο	v**oo**tero
Cheese feta	τυρί φέτα	tee**ree** **fe**ta
French fries	πατάτες τηγανιτές	pat**a**tes teegan**ee**tes

Greek Salad • Onions, tomatoes and olives
with olive oil   χωριάτικη σαλάτα   hory**ia**teekee sal**a**ta

Olive oil	λάδι	l**a**thee
Olives	ελιές	el**ee**es

Melitzanasalata • An appetizer sauce made
of eggplant, garlic   μελιτζανασαλάτα   meleezanasal**a**ta

Rice	ρύζι	r**ee**zee
Taramasalata • Cod roe dip	ταραμασαλατα	taramasal**a**ta

Tzatziki • A sauce made from cucumbers, garlic,
yogurt and olive oil   τζατζίκι   tzatz**ee**kee

Desserts

Baklavas • Phyllo pastry roll filled with nuts and topped with
syrup.   μπακλαβάς   bakl**a**vas

Galakobouriko • Phyllo pastry filled with custard and topped
with syrup.   γαλατομπούρικο   galatob**oo**reeko

Granita	γρανίτα	gran**ee**ta
Ice cream	παγωτό	pag**o**to

Kataifi • Shredded phyllo pastry roll filled with nuts and
topped with syrup.   κατάϊφι   kata**ee**fee

Karithopita • Walnut cake   καρυδόπιτα   karee**tho**peeta

Loukoumades • Fried dough balls, topped with syrup and
cinnamon   λουκουμάδες   lookoo**ma**thes

Loukoumi • Turkish Delight Candy
    λουκούμι   look**oo**mee

Rice pudding	ρυζόγαλο	reez**o**galo
Yogurt with honey	γιαούρτι με μέλι	yia**oo**rtee me m**e**lee

Footsteps Through Athina

Fruit

Apple	μήλο	meelo
Apricot	βερύκοκο	vereekoko
Banana	μπανάνα	banana
Cherry	κεράσι	kerasee
Fig	σύκο	seeko
Grapefruit	γκρέιπφρουτ	grapefruit
Grapes	σταφύλια	stafeeleea
Lemon	λεμόνι	lemonee
Melon	πεπόνι	peponee
Orange	πορτοκάλι	portokalee
Peach	ροδάκινο	rothakeeno
Pear	αχλάδι	ahlathee
Pineapple	άνανας	ananas
Plum	δαμάσκηνο	thamaskeeno
Strawberry	φράουλα	fraoola
Watermelon	καρπούζι	karpoozee

Vegetables

Carrot	καρότο	karoto
Cucumber	αγγούρι	angoori
Eggplant	μελιτζάνα	meleetzana
French Fries	πατάτες τηγανιτές	patates teeganeetes
Lettuce	μαρούλι	maroolee
Onion	κρυμμύδι	kremeethi
Peas	αρακάς	arakas
Pepper	πιπεριά	peepereea
Potato	πατάτα	patata
Tomato	ντομάτα	domata
Salad	σαλάτα	salata
Spinach	σπανάκι	spanaki
Zucchini	κολοκύθι	kolokeethee

184

FOOTSTEPS THROUGH ATHINA

Beverages

Beer	μπύρα	beera
Coca Cola	κόκα κόλα	Koka kola
Coffee	καφές	kafes
Greek coffee	ελληνικός καφές	Elleeneekos kafes
Iced Coffee	φραπέ	frape
Lemonade	λεμονάδα	lemonatha
Milk	γάλα	gala
Orange Juice	χυμός πορτακάλι	heemos portokalee
Orangeade	πορτοκαλάδα	portokalatha
Tea	τσάι	tsaee
Water	νερό	nero
Wine	κρασί	krasee

Days

Monday	Δευτέρα	Theftera
Tuesday	Τρίτη	Treetee
Wednesday	Τετάρτη	Tetartee
Thursday	Πέμπτη	Pembtee
Friday	Παρασκευή	Paraskevee
Saturday	Σάββατο	Savvato
Sunday	Κυριακή	Keereeakee

Times

What time is it?	Τι ώρα είναι;	Tee ora eene
It is two o'clock.	Είναι δύο η ώρα.	Eene deeo ee ora.
Today	σήμερα	seemera
Tonight	απόψε	apopse
Tomorrow	αύριο	avreeo
Yesterday	χθές	ekthes
Now	τώρα	tora

GREEK LANGUAGE AND EDUCATION

Footsteps Through Athina

Numbers

0		μηδέν	meethen
1		ένα	ena
2		δύο	theeo
3		τρία	treea
4		τέσσερα	tessera
5		πέντε	pende
6		έξι	eksee
7		επτά	epta
8		οκτώ	okto
9		εννέα	ennea
10		δέκα	theka
11		έντεκα	entheka
12		δώδεκα	thotheka
13		δεκατρία	thekatreea
14		δεκατέσσερα	thekatessera
15		δεκαπέντε	thekapende
16		δεκαέξι	thekaeksee
17		δεκαεπτά	thekaepta
18		δεκαοκτώ	thekaokto
19		δεκαεννέα	thekaennea
20		είκοσι	eekosee
30		τριάντα	treeanta
40		σαράντα	saranta
50		πενήντα	peneenda
60		εξήντα	ekseenda
70		εβδομήντα	evthomeenda
80		ογδόντα	ogthonda
90		ενενήντα	eneneenda
100		εκατό	ekato
200		διακόσια	theeakoseea
300		τριακόσια	treeakoseea
400		τετρακόσια	tetrakoseea
500		πεντακόσια	pentakoseea

FOOTSTEPS THROUGH ATHINA

600	εξακόσια	eksa<u>ko</u>seea
700	επτακόσια	epta<u>ko</u>sseea
800	οκτακόσια	okto<u>ko</u>seea
900	εννιακόσια	ennea<u>ko</u>seea
1000	χίλια	<u>hee</u>leea

PLACES

Bank	τράπεζα	<u>tra</u>peza
Beach	παραλία	para<u>lee</u>a
Bus Stop	στάση λεωφορείων	<u>Sta</u>see leofo<u>ree</u>on
Church	εκκλησία	ekklee<u>see</u>a
Metro Station	σταθμός μετρό	stath<u>mos</u> metro
Museum	μουσείο	moo<u>see</u>o
Restaurant	εστιατόρειο	estea<u>to</u>reeo
Store	μαγαζί	maga<u>zee</u>
Train Station	σταθμός τρένου	stath<u>mos</u> <u>tre</u>noo

TRANSPORTATION

Boat	Καράβι	ka<u>ra</u>vee
Bus	λεωφορείο	leofo<u>ree</u>o
Car	αυτοκίνητο	afto<u>kee</u>neeto
Taxi	ταξί	tak<u>see</u>
Train	τρένο	<u>tre</u>no

CLOTHING & ACCESSORIES

athletic shoes	αθλητκά παπούτσια	ath<u>lee</u>ti<u>ka</u> pa<u>poo</u>tseea
belt	ζώνη	<u>zo</u>nee
bikini	μπικίνι	bee<u>kee</u>nee
blouse	μπλούζα	<u>bloo</u>za
coat	παλτό	pal<u>to</u>
dress	φόρεμαb	<u>fo</u>rema
flip-flops	σαγιονάρες	sayeeo<u>na</u>res
hat	καπέλλο	ka<u>pe</u>llo
jacket	σακάκι	sa<u>ka</u>kee

Footsteps Through Athina

jeans	μπλου-τζην	Blue-tzeen
pants	παντελόνι	pantelonee
purse	τσάντα	tsanda
sand	πέδιλα	petheela
shirt	πουκάμισο	pookameeso
shoes	παπούτσια	papootseea
shorts	σορτς	sorts
slippers	παντόφλες	pandofles
skirt	φούστα	foosta
socks	κάλτσες	kaltses
suit (man's)	κουστούμι	kostoomi
suit (woman's)	ταγιέρ	tageeair
sunglasses	γυαλιά ηλίου	yialyeea eeleeou
sweater	πουλόβερ	pullover
sweatshirt	αθλητική μπλούζα	athleeteekee blooza
swimming trunks	μαγιώ	mayo
T-shirt	μπλουζάκι	bloozakee
tie	γραβάτα	gravata

The Jewelry Shop

jewelry shop	το κοσμηματοπωλείο	to kosmeematopoleeo
jewelry	τα κοσμήματα	ta kosmeemata
ring	το δακτυλίδι	to thakteeleethee
watch	το ρολόι	to roloee
necklace	κολιέ	koleeay
earrings	σκουλαρίκια	skoolareekeea
gold	χρυσό	hreeso
silver	ασήμι	aseemee

EDUCATION IN GREECE

Education in Greece is compulsory for all children between the ages of six and fifteen. Students attend classes five days a week with the schools operating about five or six hours a day. The responsibility of education falls under the Ministry of Education and Religious affairs. The curriculum for all levels of education is centralized and students throughout the country adhere to the national curriculum and use the prescribed textbooks designed by the Pedagogical Institute. The Greek educational system is divided into three levels as follows:

PRIMARY EDUCATION
Primary School • Dimotiko

The Greek state provides noncompulsory preschools and kindergartens throughout the country for children age four to six and many children attend these schools. Greek children begin their formal education when they are six years old. Primary school (dimotiko sxoleio) consists of six grades. Upon completion of grade six, the students receive a certificate.

SECONDARY EDUCATION
Lower Secondary Education - Gymnasium • Junior High School

After primary school, Greek children enter the Gymnasium (gymnasio). It consists of three grades. Upon completion, the students receive a certificate that enables them to continue their studies in either a technical school or Senior high school (lykeio-lyceum).

Higher Secondary Lyceum • Senior High School

The last tier of secondary education occurs at the Lyceum (lykeio). It also consists of three grades. The students are tested on all subjects at the end of the school year. Upon completing the last year of the Lyceum, students are given nationwide examinations known as the Pan Hellenic Examinations. These exams are very difficult and competitive and students begin studying for them a year in advance. The examination results determine whether the student can enter a school of higher education.

Tertiary • Higher Education

Students interested in furthering their education can study at a vocational or technical institution, or one of the twenty-two universities in Greece.

Private Education

Article 16 of the Greek constitution allows the establishment and operation of private elementary and secondary schools. Both Greek and foreign born children are enrolled at many of these schools. All private elementary and secondary schools are required to follow the Greek national curriculum and use the same textbooks as the public schools, unless the schools are independently and privately run, such as international schools. To date, the Greek government does not recognize private universities in Greece and students with foreign university degrees obtained from such institutions are not allowed to work in the public sector. Foreigners living in Greece have the opportunity to study in private American and English schools consisting of elementary and secondary school, colleges and universities. Let's take a look at a few of the well known American Schools in Greece.

American Community School of Athens
ACS · Halandri

The origin of ACS dates back to 1946, at the end of the Second World War when the first school (then named the British Army School) opened in Glyfada primarily for the children of British personnel stationed in Greece. Shortly after its opening, a number of American children who had arrived in Greece also enrolled at the school. A high school was soon established in Kolonaki and later moved to the suburb of Kiffisia. Eventually, branches of the primary schools were opened in Psychiko and Filothei. The school was then renamed the Anglo American School. In the 1954-1955 school year, the school was chartered in the state of Delaware as a non-profit educational institution for children of diplomatic and army personnel and was renamed the American Community School of Athens. In 1960, the school received funds to purchase property in Halandri and in 1963 the Greek government officially licensed the school to provide education to American children.

The next few decades saw the expansion of new school buildings equipped with the state-of-the-art facilities. ACS was recently authorized by the Greek Ministry of Education to offer classes and examinations leading to the Apolitirio, the Greek High School degree. Now, six decades after its founding, ACS continues to offer outstanding instruction and superb athletic, cultural and programs in an exquisite, high-tech environment.

Footsteps Through Athina

Deree College • American College of Greece • Agia Paraskevi

Looking to attend a college in Greece? Well here is a magnificent, distinctive, liberal arts college that provides one of the best American educations in a Greek setting! And trust me, I can vow to this since Deree is my alma mater!

The institute was first founded in 1875 by American missionaries in Smyrna, Asia Minor and was named the American Collegiate Institute. It served as an all-girls high school consisting of a department of general studies and a teachers training center. Lessons were conducted in English and also in Greek, Armenian and Turkish to accommodate the ethnic diversity of the community. It was considered to be one of the finest schools in Asia Minor where several prominent Greek women studied.

In 1885, the College expanded to an institution of higher education and functioned until 1922, when the Asia Minor Catastrophe forced it to close. The building served as place of refuge for students and their families until it was destroyed by the great fire that swept throughout the town. This horrifying event resulted in the expulsion of one third of the Greek population from Asia Minor, the majority fleeing to resettle in Greece. Having recognized the importance of this fine institution, Prime Minister Eleftherios Venizelos granted the college permission to purchase land and reopen as the American Junior College for Girls in Old Phaleron, Athens. As enrollment increased, a new school was established in Hellinkon and renamed Orlinda Childs Pierce College.

During the Second World War, the college was forced to temporarily close down and the school was used as a military hospital. Classes were conducted in the homes of faculty and students. It opened again in 1946 under the name of the American College for Girls. Over time, there were significant developments at the college. The upper division of the college was authorized to grant a Bachelor of Science degree in business administration and a Bachelor of Arts degree in the liberal arts. The secondary school division was granted and recognized as a six year Greek national high school recognized by the Greek government.

In 1965, the campus relocated to Agia Paraskevi on the western slopes of Mt. Hymettus. The undergraduate division was soon renamed Deree College. In 1979 Pierce College and Deree College became known as the American College of Greece. Over time, numerous changes occurred within the college, thanks to President John Bailey, who served as president for thirty three years. Among these were: the acquirement of a downtown campus; the establishment of an MBA program; and accreditation with the New England Association of Schools and Colleges. The college recently acquired the Plaka building, a renovated neoclassical structure in the historical Plaka district.

Today the institution is comprised of the following divisions:
- Pierce College - secondary division, high school and lyceum
- Deree Junior College - two year associate program located in downtown Athens campus building
- Deree, upper division - two campuses, Agia Paraskevi and downtown Athens

During the past few decades, the luxurious, 65-acre campus has grown in size and is today one of the most magnificent campuses in Greece. Upon entering the main building, we approach classrooms that open out into airy courtyards. The building also contains modern Science and Psychology labs, an ultra modern library containing more than 80,000 volumes and special collections with private study rooms, computer research stations, a media center and much more. The state-of-the-art facilities contribute to the school's academic achievements.

If you are hungry you can get a bite to eat in the student lounge and treat yourself to some of Greece's very best- Goodies, the famous place for hamburgers, or FloCafe, the biggest coffee chain in Greece. If you would rather drink your coffee by taking in the magnificent view of Athens, you can stop at the campus Starbucks coffee shop, which is situated on a small hill near the entrance of this building. It is also near the college museum that  houses the memorabilia of the history of the college.

Interested in athletics? The athletic centers are among the best in Greece, boasting an Olympic sized heated swimming pool, outdoor facilities for tennis, basketball, soccer and track and a new  gymnasium. The school was the proud host to many USA Olympic teams that trained at the College during the Athens 2004 Olympics.

The byzantine-style chapel of the Three Hierarchs proudly stands on a slope overlooking the campus. Several students and faculty have used this chapel for weddings and baptisms.

For entertainment, the college offers a variety of events ranging from instrumental to choral music presentations, lectures, film previews, ballet performances and much more. You can  choose to attend a performance on campus at one of the two theaters: the Pierce Theater and the Studio Theater, or the indoor amphitheater. In addition, you can attend a performance at the open air theater that resembles an ancient Greek theater and provides a spectacular view to the Attica basin. The downtown campus theater also offers a wide range of performances.

GREEK CULTURE

From its beginning in antiquity to this very day, Greece has been a land so rich in its traditions and customs. Greeks are particularly proud of their heritage and culture. Their sense of *Greekness* is

strongly imbedded in their minds and habits, and truly defines their national belonging and ethnic identity. It is an intricate part of their daily life and lived with an intense passion. You can see traces of Greek culture and tradition everywhere; much of which has its roots in the Greek Orthodox religion, but often times stemming back to the Turkish era or even antiquity.

Hopefully you will be in Greece for a Greek holiday or festivity so that you can experience the true warmth of Greek hospitality and celebration. Whether it is an ethnic holiday, a name day, a wedding or a baptism, there always seems to be an occasion to celebrate in Greece. And these celebrations are

exuberant! Let's take a look at some of the traditional festivities that play an important part in every Greek's life and see what makes them so special.

GREEK HOLIDAYS
JANUARY
NEW YEARS - FEAST OF ST. BASIL: This holiday is associated with a new beginning. Families gather together to cut and eat the *Vassilopita* (Basil's cake), a tradition that originates from Byzantium. The person who finds the hidden coin in his/her slice is said to have good luck throughout the year. Some other New Year's traditions include: The *podariko*, in which the first person to enter the house steps in with his/her right foot, carrying an icon or a pomegranate, *rodi*, that he

or she breaks for good luck. Gifts are exchanged on this day rather than on Christmas.

EPHIFANY - JANUARY 6: This is a very important day because it commemorates Christ's baptism in the Jordan River. In every part of Greece where there is a sea, lake, or river, you will most likely find a priest throwing a cross into the water and young men diving in to retrieve it. He who finds it is considered to be very blessed.

FEBRUARY

CARNIVAL OR APOKREAS: Depending on the Orthodox calendar, this celebration usually takes place in February. For three consecutive weeks before the beginning of lent, people celebrate by dressing up in costumes and masks and by attending parties or going to tavernas to sing, dance and party with friends. It is a very fun time of year. In the city of Patra, a very big carnival parade is held with magnificent floats and festivities.

KATHARI DEUFTERA - CLEAN MONDAY:

This is the first day of Lent, *Sarakosti*, that will last for forty days. Many Greeks begin fasting (*nistia*) and give up meat and dairy products for the entire Lenten season. In preparation, people gather together for a big Lenten meal called *Koulouma*. Many families go on a picnic. They eat special bread called *lagana* that is thin, flat and sprinkled with a lot of sesame seeds. *Halvah* (a sweet made with sesame pulp called *tahini*), pickles, olives and octopus are also part of the meal. Children fly kites, especially on Philopappos Hill. Prizes are given for the most beautiful and original kites and also for the one that flies the highest.

MARCH

MARCH 1 - MARCH BRACELET – MARTIS: On this day, it is customary for mothers to braid and place red and white string bracelets called *Martis* on their children's wrists. The colors red and white symbolize red cheeks and a white complexion. This is a superstition believing that children who wear the bracelet will be protected against having their cheeks burned by the sun. The bracelets are worn until the Resurrection Service on Holy Saturday.

25 MARTIOU - MARCH 25TH GREEK INDEPENDENCE DAY & ANNUNCIATION OF THE VIRGIN MARY (EVANGELISMOS):
March 25th is a double feast day historically and ecclesiastically. It commemorates the liberation of the Greeks in 1821 from the Turks who occupied the country for nearly four hundred years. There are many parades throughout the country in which Greek school children march in their ethnic costumes. It also marks the celebration of the Annunciation of the Virgin Mary. Special church services are held in commemoration of both of these big events.

APRIL OR MAY (DEPENDING ON CHURCH CALENDAR)

GREEK EASTER – PASCHA: Greek Easter is the most sacred and celebrated religious holiday for Greek Orthodox Christians and nowhere else in the world can the Easter spirit be felt more than in Greece. Every year my mind wanders back to the many Easters I spent there and fond memories reappear. The smell of Easter bread and sweets baking in ovens; the scent of burning candles and incense; priests chanting; church bells ringing; red paper Mache Easter eggs hanging in bakery shop windows together with decorated Easter *Lambathes* (candles) waiting to be bought for that special child. These are just a few of my special memories of Easter in Greece.

Holy week is very inspiring in the Orthodox Church and if you get a chance to attend a service it certainly will have a profound affect on you. Here is a description of the observances and traditions that take place during Megali Ebdomada - Holy Week:

SATURDAY OF LAZARUS: This is a day of great joy and reverence that celebrates the resurrection of Lazarus. It is the only time in the church year that the resurrection service is celebrated on a day other than Easter. In many villages, women bake small breads called

Footsteps Through Athina

lazarakia that are shaped in the form of a human body. Children go from house to house singing a song about the resurrection of Lazarus.

PALM SUNDAY - KYRIAKI TO VAGION: This day marks the start of Holy Week and commemorates Jesus Christ's entrance into Jerusalem. After the liturgy, the priest distributes palms that have been braided into crosses along with a branch of bay leaves to all of those in attendance at church. Once the parishioners return home, they place these Holy items in their *Iconstasion* (icon stand) for the remainder of the year.

HOLY MONDAY - MEGALI DEFTERA: Easter preparations still remain to be an important part of Greek culture. Beginning on Monday, housewives diligently clean their houses, prepare delicacies and shop for gifts, special Easter attire and food for the big day. In the evening many people attend church.

TUESDAY - MEGALI TRITI: During the day, many women make their *koulouria* - braided butter Easter cookies. In the evening, people go to church to listen to the special hymn of the *Kassiani*.

WEDNESDAY - MEGALI TETARTI - SERVICE OF THE HOLY UNCTION: Another important church day in which everyone receives the sacrament of Holy Unction (the Holy Oil) for the forgiveness of their sins.

THURSDAY - MEGALI PEMPTI: As in the past on Holy Thursday,  women make their red Easter eggs symbolizing the blood of Christ and the renewal of life. They also make *Tsourekia* (Greek Easter bread). In the evening, people attend church to hear the twelve excerpts of the four gospels relating Christ's Passion. This is a very long and solemn service. After the first six are read, a large wooden cross with a carved statue of Christ is brought out and placed in front of the altar. Young girls remain at church to decorate the *Epitaphios*, the bier of Christ, with garlands of white and purple flowers.

GOOD FRIDAY - MEGALI PARASKEVI - TO EPITAPHIO: This is  the most sacred and solemn day of Holy Week. During the morning *Apolkathalis* service, the priest removes the body of Christ from the cross. This figure is covered with a cloth and kept in the Holy Altar for fifty days. Church bells ring in mourning throughout the entire day. In the evening the procession of the *Epitaphio*, representing Christ's funeral takes place. A band or choir playing solemn hymns precedes the procession followed by cantors, clergy, women bearing myrrh, altar boys and the people from the congregation who carry a lit candle. People scatter flowers and perfume on the *Epitaphio*. In Greece, the *Epitaphio* is taken out of the church and carried through the streets of the neighborhood.

HOLY SATURDAY - MEGALO SAVATO: During the afternoon, the  Holy Light or Eternal Flame arrives in Greece from Jerusalem on a Greek Military jet. If you happen to be in Greece, you can view this event on Greek television. You will see several priests waiting at the airport with lanterns to take this light to their churches for the Resurrection service. This is a very busy day, especially for the women who are engaged at making the traditional Easter soup, *Mageiritsa* (herbs and intestines) and preparing other delicacies for the Easter feast. Late in the evening, at about 11 pm, everyone (young and old) sets out for church. Since the churches have limited space, the majority of people gather in the church courtyard holding a white, unlit candle. Children dressed in their special Easter attire proudly carry their decorated Easter *lambatha* (candle) from their godparents. Shortly before midnight, all of the church lights are turned off except for the Holy Flame that is inside the altar. The dark church symbolizes the darkness and silence of Christ's tomb. Everyone waits in anticipation for the clock to strike midnight. Before midnight, the priest lights his candle from the Holy Light. He then offers it to the congregation. He chants "*Defte Lavete Fos*", "Come

Footsteps Through Athina

Take the Holy Light". One by one the candles are lit, illuminating both the church and courtyard. The priest proceeds to a platform outside the church with the holy icon of the Resurrection and the Holy Light. At midnight, he loudly calls out *"Christos Anesti",* "Christ is Risen". Everyone responds with the words, *"Alithos Anesti",* "Truly He is Risen!" The congregation and priest continue to chant *Christos Anesti - Alithos Anesti.* In Greece, it is customary at this point to ignite fireworks. Everyone greets and wishes each other *"Kalo Pascha",* "Happy Easter". After the service, families return home to break the fast. It is considered lucky to reach home with a lit candle and then make the sign of the cross three times over the front door of the house. When this is done, families gather together for the festive Resurrection dinner: lamb, mageiritsa soup, red Easter eggs, and Greek *koulourakia* (Easter butter cookies). One of the oldest Greek Easter traditions is the *Tsougrisma*, the cracking of the red eggs in which everyone has an egg and tries to break the ends of others' eggs. The person with the unbroken egg will have good luck throughout the year.

EASTER SUNDAY - PASCHA: Throughout the country, people get up early in the morning to prepare lamb on the spit for the big Easter feast. In the afternoon, a second resurrection takes place in church at the Service of Love. The gospel is read and translated into seven languages. People continue to greet each other with the special Easter expressions *"Christos Anesti"* and *"Alithos Anesti".* This is truly the biggest day of celebrations and the festivities will continue until late at night. All homes are open to welcome guests who arrive with cookies, eggs and sweets. The smell of the delicious Greek cuisine lingers through the air together with Greek music accompanied by dancing and singing. Television programs broadcast celebrations with several famous singers entertaining and joining in the festive atmosphere that is so vivid across all of Greece.

MAY

MAY DAY - PROTO MAGIA: The first of May is a national holiday in Greece with parades and other festivities. It traditionally marks the feast of flowers. Many families have picnics in the country and pick wild flowers which are woven into a wreath. The wreaths are then hung on balconies and over doorways until the feast day of St. John on June 24th, and are then often burned in bonfires. The wreaths are considered to ward off evil and usher in spring. This is a magnificent time of the year; the country is surrounded by colorful, blossoming flowers that fill the air with tantalizing, aromatic fragrances and fields overrun by my favorite red *Paparounes*, poppies!

Anastenaria are fire-walking ceremonies that are held in honor of the Saints Agios Konstantinos and Agia Eleni (May 21). People walk and dance across burning coals embracing icons of the two saints. This ritual has its origins in antiquity and is associated with the god of Dionysios. The event takes place mainly in Serres and Langada outside of Thessaloniki (northern Greece).

JUNE

As summer draws near, Greek children anticipate the end of classes and the beginning of vacation. Elementary schools across the nation have an end of the year program in which the children sing, present poems and plays and celebrate the finishing of the school year.

JULY

Greek summer is magnificent; carefree days of swimming, eating fantastic fresh food outdoors, vacationing, attending *Panagiri's*, taking strolls and enjoying all that the country has to offer.

AUGUST

PANAGIA - ASSUMPTION OF THE VIRGIN MARY - THEKAPENAVGOUSTOS AUGUST 15: This is a very important religious holiday in Greece. It commemorates the dormition and the falling asleep of the *Panagia,* Virgin Mary. There is a big exodus out of the main cities as it is customary for Greeks to return to their hometown and celebrate this day with family and friends.

SEPTEMBER

14 SEPTEMBER – EXALTATION OF THE HOLY CROSS: This feast commemorates the triumph of the cross by which Christ redeemed the world. The cross was miraculously found on September 14, 326 AD by Saint Helen, the mother of Constantine, while she was on a pilgrimage to Jerusalem. This day is considered to be the last of the major summer holidays even though it takes place in fall.

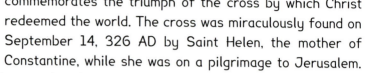

School resumes – After the feast day of the Holy Cross, schools in Greece resume once again. After having enjoyed the pleasures of the Greek summer, children return with their new backpacks and supplies. On the first day of school it is customary to have an *Agiasmos* service in which the priest sprinkles Holy Water with a cross and basil and blesses the children, teachers and the school.

OCTOBER

OXI DAY – NO DAY – OCTOBER 28: Oxi Day commemorates the anniversary when former general and Prime Minister Metaxas said *"No"* to Benito Mussolini's request to allow Italian forces to enter Greece at the beginning of World War II. The small Greek army drove the Italian army back into Albania. On this day, big parades take place in Athens and Thessaloniki. Soldiers, tanks, armored vehicles and schoolchildren dressed in ethnic costumes all take part in this event. At school celebrations, the children also recite poems and songs and repeat the word "OXI" with much pride.

NOVEMBER

With the exception of a few name days (Feast Day of the Archangels Michael & Gabriel and St. Andrew), there are no ethnic

holidays during the month of November. The weather in Greece is beginning to get colder and as you are walking around in Athens you will notice and get a whiff of the chestnuts roasting on sidewalk stands. They taste great, so don't hesitate to try some.

DECEMBER

ST. NICHOLAS - AGIOS NIKOLAOS: December 6th, this feast day  commemorates St. Nicholas, the saint of sailors, travelers, merchants and children. According to tradition, his clothes are drenched with brine, his beard is dripping with seawater and his face is all sweaty since he has been working hard to rescue sinking ships against the dangerous waves. On any ship in Greece, you will find an icon of this saint who is protecting it from danger. Numerous processions take place around the sea and chapels are named after him. This date marks the beginning of the Christmas season. Many people exchange gifts on this day.

CHRISTMAS EVE - PARAMONI XRISTOUGENNON: On this day, the streets come alive as children travel from house to house singing the *Kalanda* (Christmas carols relating to the birth of Christ) and offering good wishes to all. They carry metal triangles, little clay drums, and often a boat representing the sea and fish (life giving gifts of Christ). The children are rewarded with sweets, dried fruit and coins.

CHRISTMAS - TA XRISTOUGENNA: Christmas in Greece is considered to be the second most important holiday after Easter. It is not as big of a holiday as in other countries; however, throughout the last decade it has become much more commercialized than in the past. There are many unique Greek customs and traditions associated with this holiday.

Christmas Day is a very special family day and, as you can guess, there is a big celebration. After church, the families return home to a huge feast. The Greek Christmas meal is made up of several delicacies. Although in the past pork was considered the main meal, it has now been replaced with roast turkey stuffed with chestnuts, rice, and pine nuts and it is accompanied by a number of other Greek dishes. The deserts are phenomenal and include: *melomakarona* - honey dipped cookies often covered with nuts; *kourambiedes* - butter cookies dusted with powder sugar; *diples* - fried dough cookies dipped in honey; *baklava* - layers of phyllo dough filled with almonds and cinnamon and soaked in lemon syrup, and *Christostomo* (Christ's bread), a round loaf decorated with a cross on the top of the bread.

In many Greek homes it is traditional to see a shallow wooden bowl with a suspended piece of wire across the rim from which hangs a sprig of basil that is wrapped around a wooden cross. Water is kept in the bowl to keep the basil alive. Once a day, a member of the family dips the cross and basil into holy water and sprinkles water in every room of the house. This is done to keep away the *Kallikantzaroi* - mischievous little goblins that appear during the 12 day period from Christmas to Epiphany (January 6). Legend states they are afraid of Holy Water. It is believed that these creatures emerge from the center of the earth and slip through chimneys, so many people try to avoid them by keeping their fire places burning day and night for twelve days.

NEW YEAR'S EVE - PARAMONI PROTOXRONIAS: Once again,

children go around the neighborhood singing the *Kalanda* (carols), but this time the songs are related to St. Basil and the New Year. In the past, they always carried a boat, but today this tradition is not as common. Just as with Christmas, the children are also rewarded for their caroling with candy, fruit and coins. In the evening, there are many parties taking place. Some people go out to clubs and restaurants. It is tradition, especially among the elders, to play cards on New Year's Eve. Of course, the winner is considered to bring in the New Year with much luck.

FOOTSTEPS THROUGH ATHINA

TRADITIONAL SYMBOLIC ARTIFACTS

As you are traveling throughout Greece, you will notice many traditional objects in stores, houses and buildings. You probably are wondering what they symbolize, so let me explain some of these to you.

KOMBOLOI : You will see several young and old Greek men (women have also joined the group) walking with beads in their hands. You may also notice that they are hanging around the mirror in cars and trucks. What are they? They are called *komboloi,* or worry beads, and are considered to be a fidget toy that relieves stress and boredom. There are different modes of swinging the beads and the movement often signifies the person's mood. Although *komboloi* resemble prayer beads or a rosary, they have no religious connection. In fact, you might run across a number of priests that are playing with them as well.

The origin of the *komboloi* is often debated. Some say that they derived from *Kombosini* - Greek prayer beads used by Orthodox monks. Others say that they stem from an Islamic tradition. The word "komboloi" derives from the Greek words *kombos*, meaning knot, and *loi*, meaning a group that sticks together. *Komboloi* are strung on either a cord or chain. Most *komboloi* consist of a strand of about sixteen to twenty beads. The top bead is tied and usually adorned with a tassel.

Komboloi are quite popular in Greece and come in a variety of colors, sizes and prices (ranging from $5 to $350). They make a great gift so be sure to pick up a few of them. You can find them anywhere, from tourist stores to *periptera* (kiosks). If you happen to be in Nafplion, Greece, you can visit the unique Komboloi Museum. It is the only one in the country and houses quite a collection.

FOOTSTEPS THROUGH ATHINA

GREEK SUPERSTITIONS

MATI - THE EVIL EYE: The Greeks wear them around their necks, they are hung in car and store windows, the souvenir shops sell them attached to ribbons, icons and other paraphernalia; those blue  glass eyes ranging in a number of sizes are all over the place. So, you ask, what are they? They are called evil eyes and are supposed to protect you against evil. It is part of a Greek superstition that stems back to the time of paganism in Greece. Paintings of Greek *triremes* (a class of warships used in ancient Greece) portray the evil eye on the front of warships. This superstition is still very alive in Greece and in countries around the Mediterranean Sea.

So what actually is the *Mati*, evil eye? It is a negative power that we all unconsciously carry within ourselves even if we don't want to admit it. When we stare at a person for too long, either in admiration or envy, or give a compliment to someone, we can give off a bad spell. The victim will suddenly feel ill. Symptoms can include dizziness, a headache, fainting and even death. You wonder how anyone in today's society can believe this; well, don't try arguing this with a Greek! The majority of people will insist it is true and, believe me, they will have many stories to share with you. Even the Greek Orthodox Church believes in these evil forces; however, while believing that the actual blue *mati* amulet cannot be a stronger protector than a cross that one wears and that the cross

 should not be worn with a *mati*, the church does believe that one can be possessed by this evilness. In fact, it is referred to as "*Vaskania*" in the church.

So how can one get rid of the evil eye? Although the Orthodox Church believes that only a priest can remove this power by a special reading and prayer, many Greeks go against this practice. There are many women who have learned from their mothers how to rid

Footsteps Through Athina

Greek Culture

one of this evil spell. The first step is to see if one is really possessed or just plain tired. This is done by dropping a few drops of oil in a glass of water. If the oil drops to the bottom of the glass, this person has the evil eye. A prayer is then read to the one with the evil eye.

How can you ward off the evil eye? There are a few steps that you can take. The first is to wear a blue evil eye trinket. The color blue and the painted glass eye (which can reflect) are both thought to ward off evil. Even a blue bead can serve the purpose. It is also commonly thought that a blue eyed person can give off the evil eye - so be careful when those with blue eyes give compliments. Since many Greek people are afraid that their compliments will have a negative consequence, they often spit three times or say "*ptew ptew*" when delivering their good wishes.

Even at a Greek Orthodox baptism, the priest will blow into the air three times to glorify the Holy Trinity and then spit onto the ground three times at the devil.

Women, children and babies are most likely to be victims of the Evil Eye and you will notice that the majority of babies have an evil eye attached to their clothing. They can also be wearing a *filaxto* (a sachet containing something Holy or blessed) on the back of their clothing. Garlic is also used for the evil eye, for warding off the devil and for good luck. You may notice a strand of garlic hanging in one's house or place of business. Many Greeks also carry a piece of garlic in their pocket. So the next time that you are feeling a bit under the weather, think twice! It may be the evil eye. As long as you are in Greece, stock up on a few. They make fun gifts and also serve as great protector against this evil force.

TUESDAY - TRITI: In Greece, Tuesday is considered to be an unlucky day since on Tuesday May 29th, 1453, the city of Constantinople fell to the Ottoman Turks. Greeks will not start a new business on this day and several people also refuse to travel on Tuesdays. Although the number 13 is considered to be lucky in

FOOTSTEPS THROUGH ATHINA

Greece (it represents Christ and the twelve disciples), if it falls on a Tuesday, it then is viewed as being an unlucky day.

SALT: It is believed that salt has great powers and is a purifying  force. Therefore there is a number of Greek superstitions in which salt is an important source. It is used to ward off the devil and demons by throwing it over your left shoulder. When someone moves into a new house, salt will be sprinkled throughout the rooms to remove any evil spirit. It can also be used to get rid of unwanted guests by either sprinkling it on their chair or by throwing it behind them.

ITCHY HAND: If you have an itchy hand in Greece, you will either be receiving or giving away money. If it is your right hand that itches, you will receive money. If it is your left hand, you will give money. If both hands itch, you will both receive and give.

TOUCH RED - PIASE KOKKINO: When two people say the same word or have the same thought at the same time, they believe that it is an omen that they may get into a fight. For this reason they will say *Piase Kokkino* and touch something nearby that is red.

SNEEZING: In Greece, if you sneeze, it is believed that someone is talking about you. Since you don't know who it is, you try to figure out the person by saying peoples' names out loud. If you say the name and stop sneezing, then you have found the person. Another way to figure 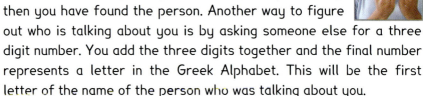 out who is talking about you is by asking someone else for a three digit number. You add the three digits together and the final number represents a letter in the Greek Alphabet. This will be the first letter of the name of the person who was talking about you.

RELIGIOUS ARTIFACTS

Greece is a land in which 98% of the people belong to the Greek Orthodox Church. Churches, crosses, religious objects; you can see

FOOTSTEPS THROUGH ATHINA

traces of religion throughout the entire country. Its influence is also very evident in many of the traditions and characteristics of the Greek people. When Greek people pass by a church, they make the sign of the cross. If you happen to be on a bus that passes by a church, take note on how many people are doing so. Many Greeks also make the sign of the cross at the start of a meal. And then there are those that will do so when traveling, as when a plane, boat or bus starts off. Orthodoxy is an integral part of every Greek home and displayed through several religious artifacts. Let's learn about some of these!

ICONS: An icon is a sacred picture of Christ or a saint adhered to a piece of wood. Every Greek Church and home is full of beautiful icons that portray a special story. You will find them in nearly every room of a house. Orthodox Christians venerate icons by kissing them. They do not worship them since they only worship God. The Orthodox religion does not believe in religious statues, so don't expect to find any in Greece.

ICONOSTASION: The *iconostasion* is a special shelf or cabinet where icons are placed. In addition, other items such as palms, flowers from Good Friday, sacramental candles, Holy water and oil, and incense burners are often placed together with the icons. The *iconostasion* may be used as a central place of prayer and worship. It is traditionally located in an area facing the East.

STEFANA & STEFANOTHEKI - WEDDING CROWN & CASES: The use of Greek wedding crowns is a tradition that originates back from ancient Greece when the couple wore *stefana*, crowns made of olive leaves, vine leaves and lemon

flowers that were dedicated to Aphrodite. The Orthodox Church still uses the crowns today that represent the connection of two people, or the rings that connect the chain of their lives. The *stefana* are tied together by a ribbon symbolizing that the couple has to remain together forever.

INCENSE BURNER - THIMIATO & INCENSE: The *Thimiato* is used for burning incense. The incense is a fragrant, inflammable piece that is placed on a small bit of burning charcoal. The pleasant fragrance intensifies the need for prayer and also dispels evil spirits. Many people light incense in front of the *iconostasion* and at the cemetery.

KANTELI - HANGING VIGIL OIL CANDLES: These beautiful hanging vigil oil candles are found in all Greek churches and in many homes. The glass cased candles that are usually hung in front of the icons stay lit with olive oil or electric power. There is a wide selection of magnificent ones in Greece. If you see one, buy it; you won't find the same selection and prices back home.

PROSKINITERIA - ROADSIDE SHRINES: You may be wondering what the small religious boxes are that are scattered among bends in the roads of Greece. The so-called *proskiniteria* are shrines that are built in remembrance of someone killed at this spot or a token of thanksgiving to someone who miraculously survived an accident at this point. They range in sizes from a mere box to the size of a small church with a cross on the top and glass windows. Families that build these shrines take very good care of them and continuously light candles and oil lamps that are placed beside the Holy icons.

Footsteps Through Athina

Traditional Greek Orthodox Ceremonies

GREEK NAME DAYS: As you already have noticed, Greeks love to celebrate! And lucky them! In addition to the yearly birthday, they also celebrate their name day. Greek name days are a very important part of Greek life. Nearly every day of the year is dedicated to a Christian saint or martyr so there is always someone – somewhere - celebrating! The Greek Orthodox Church observes the day of the saints. The name

day is the feast day of the saint for which someone is named. When a church celebrates its name day of the patron saint, it holds a big feast called a Panagiri that takes place outside of the church. There is plenty of food, music, dancing and booths that sell handmade items.

Children are usually named after the patron saint of their region. The oldest son is named after his paternal grandfather and the eldest daughter after her paternal grandmother. It is traditional for the person with the name day to host a party. The more popular the saint is, the chances are that more people have this name, which means more parties to attend. Invitations are never sent out. It is just assumed that you will stop in to wish the person celebrating a Happy Name Day. If you plan on attending a party, make sure that you go with a very hearty appetite. Trust me - there will be a lot of great Greek food. And don't forget to bring a gift!

GREEK BAPTISM & CHRISMATION: Usually around the age of

one, a Greek baby is brought to church to be baptized. One or two people, usually relatives or good friends of the family are chosen to be the godparent or godparents of the infant. This is a real honor in the church, as the godparents are considered as important, if not more so, than the actual parents. The Greek baptism is considered to be the biggest event in a Greek Orthodox person's life. And what a lovely and lavish event that it is! It is considered to be the rebirth of the baby and the birth of a new relationship with the godparents. As with all Orthodox services, the baptism, which constitutes one of the seven sacraments of the Church, is truly unique and rich in tradition. The ceremony starts off with an exorcism. The baby, priest and godparents stand in the narthex (entrance) of the church. The priest  breathes three times over the baby and makes the sign of the cross over it. One of the godparents renounces Satan by turning to the west and spitting three times. Then he/she turns to the east to accept Christ by reciting the creed. Shortly after, the baby is undressed and brought to the front of the church where the Kolimvithra, baptismal font, is filled with lukewarm water. A child stands next to the font holding a beautiful, decorated white candle called lambatha. The godparent anoints oil all over the baby's body;  a tradition originating from ancient Greece when athletes rubbed their bodies with oil for strength. The priest then immerses the baby three times into the water. Each time he will repeat the baby's name. This is the first sacrament administered to the baby. Immediately after, the priest administers the second sacrament, chrismation, by anointing the baby's face, hands and feet with miron oil. He then cuts three locks of hair off the baby. This is an expression of gratitude from the baby. Greek babies cannot have a haircut until they have been baptized. When this is over, the priest hands the baby to the godparent and he/she wraps it in a white towel. The baby is then dressed in its special baptismal clothing, vaptistika (hat, headcover, underwear, socks, shoes, and the outfit).

The godparents place a gold Orthodox cross around the baby's neck. The baby then receives the third sacrament, communion. The priest returns the baby to the parents, who first pay their respect to the new godparents. Tiny crosses attached to either a blue or pink ribbon called *martirika* are given to all of the guests who witnessed this event. As always, a big feast is held after the ceremony with plenty of food, music and dancing.

THE GREEK WEDDING – GAMOS:  A Greek wedding is a very special and unforgettable event filled with several ancient and modern traditions that make it so unique and vibrant. The ceremony consists of two parts: the Service of the Betrothal and the Ceremony of the Sacrament of Marriage. At the beginning of the service the bride and groom are handed two candles. During the betrothal service, the priest blesses the rings and after making the sign of the cross with the rings over their heads, places them on their fingers. The Ceremony of the Sacrament then follows. The crowning of the couple is the focal point of the ceremony. The bride and groom are crowned with *stefana*, thin white wreaths adjoined by a white ribbon. The *koumbaro* (best man or maid of honor) exchanges the crowns from the couples head three times. Every act of the ceremony is tripled symbolizing the Holy Spirit. After this, the Gospel is read which tells of the marriage of Cana. The bride and groom are then given wine to drink three times. Next, the priest leads the couple around the altar (again three times). The *koumbaro* follows, holding the *stefana* closely on their heads. When this is over, the priest removes the crowns and places the bible in the couple's hands. A big celebration will follow with plenty of eating, drinking and traditional Greek dancing.

BOUMBOUNIERES & KOUFETA: If you are fortunate to attend a Greek wedding or baptism, you will receive *koufeta*, sugar coated Jordan almonds wrapped in tulle netting or handkerchiefs. These are

distributed to the guests as a token of appreciation for participating on this special day. The *koufeta* are often attached to a *boumbouniera*, a lovely trinket such as a picture frame, a porcelain figure or a piece of crystal for weddings and cute objects for baptisms. Odd numbers of almonds are always used in *Koufeta*. The significance for this at a wedding is that the *koufeta* are indivisible, just as the bride and groom shall remain undivided. The sweetness of the almonds symbolizes the sweetness of the couple's future life. The hardness of the almond represents the endurance of marriage.

It is still customary for young ladies to decorate the couple's matrimonial bed with handmade linens, coins, flowers and *koufeta* (symbolizing happiness, wealth, success and fertility). A baby, preferably a boy, will be placed on the bed so that the couple will soon have a child.

Greek Dance

Greek dancing is and has been an integral part of Greek culture and life since ancient times. The great philosophers Plato and Socrates believed that every educated man should dance gracefully, for it kept the mind and body strong. Greece is one of the few countries in the world where dances are just as alive today as they were in antiquity. Greek dance is a vivid component of celebrations of the Greek people and you can see the significant role it plays at weddings, baptisms, name day celebrations and religious holidays. Greek dancing is a manifestation of self expression. The dancer can express almost any emotion through dance; joy, sadness, pride, humor, strength and more. When a Greek has *Kefi* (is feeling good), the dance will reveal this mood. There are times when one is feeling sorrow, and this too will be displayed through dancing, as Zorba the Greek did in his famous Zorba dance. When a Greek wants to show loyalty and patronage to the motherland, he/she will dance a traditional Greek dance that has been passed on from generation to generation. Such dances are learned at a very young age and will be performed constantly throughout one's life.

There are many different types of Greek dances. Some dances are regional and are danced by those originating from a specific area. Several Greek dances are circle dances that start with the right foot and move counter-clockwise. The leader of the group will be linked to the others by a handkerchief. The *kalamatianos* (originating from the town of Kalamata in the Peloponesse) is one of the most popular circle dances. It is always danced at celebrations. Often, there are Greek dances that are specifically gender oriented. Women's dances are usually slow, simple and dignified, whereas the men's dances are vigorous and portray their manhood. The *tsamikos* is the perfect example of a masculine heroic Greek dance. It is fascinating to watch young Greek men perform this dance - some even do somersaults in the air. While in Athens, try to attend a performance by the Dora Stratou Dance Troupe on Philapappos Hill. You will learn a lot about traditional and regional Greek dancing and costumes and will also enjoy the show!

GREEK FOLK COSTUMES: You probably have already seen some traditional Greek costumes in Athens while walking around the souvenir shops at Plaka or visiting the Presidential Guards at the Tomb of the Unknown Soldier. Perhaps you saw a parade in which children were dressed up in their ethnic attire or had the chance to attend a Dora Stratou Dance Performance. These costumes are both a beautiful and historical part of Greek culture. Although all Greek costumes share similar characteristics in materials, construction, parts and design, there are several regional variations and individual features that differ throughout Greece. Let's take a look at the two most common costumes: the *foustanella* and the *amalia*.

FOOTSTEPS THROUGH ATHINA

THE FOUSTANELLA: The *foustanella* is a man's costume that is worn in the Peloponnese, Attica and mainland Greece. It was worn by Greek warriors during the revolution (1821) against the Ottoman Rulers and then became the official dress of King Otto's court. It consists of a pleated white skirt that is made by triangular shaped pieces of cloth called *langolia* that are sewn together. The skirt has 400 pleats, symbolizing the years during which Greece was under the Ottoman rule. The costume also has a white shirt with very wide, flowing sleeves, a *fermeli* - an embroidered woolen black or blue vest - a sash that is worn around the waist and *tsarouhia* - pointed shoes with big pompoms.

THE AMALIA: The *amalia* is the women's national costume of Greece that was adopted by Amalia, the first queen of Greece. The costume consists of a light blue, long satin skirt; burgundy-reddish velvet embroidered long sleeved jacket, a lace blouse and a woolen fez with a gold cord.

HANDICRAFTS: In addition to souvenirs and trinkets,

keep in mind that Greece is known for its unique handicrafts. These include handmade embroidered and lace works ranging from linens, clothing, and decorative tablecloths, sheets and pillows. You can also pick up exquisite jewelry, woodcarved items, traditional ceramics and great pieces of metalwork.

THE GREEK FLAG

The Greek flag is seen on buildings, cars, store windows, everywhere. The Greeks are very proud of their *Galanolfei*, blue and white flag! It originally consisted of a blue square with a diagonal cross. Today, the cross is in the upper left corner and symbolizes the Orthodox Christian faith. Nine stripes run horizontally across the flag. Each stripe denotes a symbol in the Greek motto of freedom: "E-LEY-THE RI-A-I-THA-NA-TOS", which means "Freedom or Death". This was the popular saying during the Greek War of Independence against the Turks who had occupied their land for nearly four hundred years. During the war, Andreas Londros raised the flag over the town of Voritisas in the Northern Peloponnese. The color blue stands for the beautiful Greek sea and the white stands for freedom, something that was and is so precious for the Greek people after being occupied for so many centuries.

Greek Music

It is difficult to imagine Greeks living without music. Wherever you go, you are bound to hear some type of music, whether it is traditional folkloric, Byzantine Church, modern day or some other type. Music has been imbedded in the Greek culture since antiquity and if you closely examine Greek artifacts you will see that several pieces display the gods and goddesses partaking in music and dance.

Greek music is very unique and exemplifies the centuries of historical and geographical influences that Greece experienced. When you listen to the music, you most likely will be able to associate the Turkish and Arabic flavor that is present in so many songs. Let's take a look at some different types of music that exists.

TRADITIONAL FOLK MUSIC: There are two types: *akritic* and *klephtic*. Akritic music originates from the era of the Byzantine Empire (9th-10th centuries AD) and symbolizes the frontier guards of the Empire. Klephtic music revolves around the Greek War of

Footsteps Through Athina

Independence period and expresses the people's struggle for freedom, together with their feelings for love and death.

CANTATHES: These songs originated during the 19th century and were influenced by Italian music.

RHEMBETIKO: This often gloomy music emerged among convicts, drug addicts, and dock workers. It became popular among the working class during the 1940's and 1950's. The music incorporates the bouzouki, baglamas and guitar.

TSIFTETELI: This is Greek belly-dance music that was brought over to Greece from the refugees from Asia Minor in the 1920's. You can really hear the Arabic and Turkish influence with this music.

LAIKA MUSIC: The popular music of the people. Greece has many fine singers and their music is played everywhere.

BOUZOUKI MUSIC: Chances are you have often heard Bouzouki

music. *Zorba the Greek* is one of the most famous examples of it. The origin of bouzouki music is Turkish, for the bouzouki is really a Turkish instrument called *bozuk*. It became associated with rembetiko music in Greece and then started becoming popular when the renowned Manos Hatjidakis started using it in his compositions.

Greek music is so delightful to hear, and it is catchy. You don't even have to understand the words; it just grows on you. Before leaving Greece, be sure to pick up some CD's to bring back home. I guarantee, it's the perfect way to perk you up when feeling a bit down or homesick for Greece.

 **HELPFUL GREEK WORDS**

Να Ζήσετε • Na <u>Zees</u>ete • May you long live (We say this to a bride and groom).

Να σας Ζήσει • Na sas <u>zees</u>ee • May he/she live for you (We say this to the parents, grandparents, godparents of a baby at the baptism

Χρόνια πολλά • <u>Hron</u>eea Polla • Many years; a wish for holidays and name days.

FOOTSTEPS THROUGH ATHINA

THE GREEK CUISINE · ELLINIKI KOUZINA

GREEK CUISINE

The delicious Greek cuisine; tasty, fresh, and aromatic! Sharing commonalities with other Mediterranean countries, it uses the freshest and healthiest ingredients from land and sea. Olive oil, spices, grains and bread, wine, fish, vegetables and various meats are the main elements used in the meals. And besides being delicious, the Greek cuisine is rich in vitamins and proteins, making it extremely healthy.

Greek cooking is intertwined with its history. Much of its cuisine can be traced back to ancient Greece, and to various groups that invaded the country such as the Romans, Venetians, Balkans, Turks and Slavs. In fact, many of the traditional foods have Turkish, Arabic and Persian names. Although many of the dishes are similar to those in other Mediterranean countries, Greek food is diverse having unique regional specialties and variations.

In addition to using fresh ingredients, the most characteristic elements of Greek cooking are olive oil and the herbs and spices that are collected from mountains and the countryside which are renowned for their taste, scent and healing properties. While traveling through the country, especially in mountain villages, you will encounter outdoor markets selling bags of basil, bay leaves, nutmeg, cinnamon, oregano, sage, thyme and so much more. You can also find all these at stores and supermarkets in Athens. Pick up a few to bring home the taste and scent of Greece!

Greek olive oil, *lathi*, is an essential ingredient in Greek cooking and is abundantly present in almost all Greek meals. Besides enhancing and flavoring food, several studies have shown that there are many benefits of using olive oil in food. People in countries such as Greece live a longer life with fewer health problems. Greece is one of the top three olive oil producing countries in the world thanks to the fine quality and taste of the oil. The best olive oil comes from the Peloponnese region and western

Footsteps Through Athina

Crete. As you can guess, Greece is also famous for its *elies*, olives. Most people are unaware that there is a large variety of different types of olives in Greece. They come from all different regions and are named after the region they come from. Each region has its own way of making olives, so the taste will definitely vary! Don't forget to try some; Greek olives are delicious.

Another delicacy that you absolutely must try is Greek *yiaourti*, yogurt. Made from sheep's milk (although cow's milk is often used), Greek yogurt is very creamy; much different from what you find back home. The reason for  this is that the liquid is strained, making it thick, velvety and tasty. You can often find fresh, homemade yogurt sold in round ceramic pots. It's great when served the traditional way with *meli*, Greek wild thyme honey, drizzled on top. Greek honey is unique, very healthy and world famous. Greek dishes use a lot of it for sweets and other delicacies.

Greece is also known for its *feta* cheese which is the key ingredient in Greek salads and several entrees. Made from sheep or goat milk or a combination of both, feta is usually aged over 90 days and then packed in brine. It has a rather salty, acidic taste and strong flavor. Some people have a hard time getting use to its unique taste but hopefully you won't! You can find a number of different types of this cheese ranging from soft, mild and mixed spice varieties at any supermarket.

For those of you who like to eat *kreas*, meat, you will be happy to know that it is one of the main foods in the Greek diet and used in several dishes. Wherever you go you will notice that *urni*, lamb, is quite popular in Greece. It is one of the traditional meats of Greek holidays and festivals. Since lamb and goats are free-grazing in pastures full of rich herbs, the meat has a unique taste. If you don't like eating lamb, don't worry; you can find pork, beef and poultry on all Greek menus. And don't forget there is always *souvlaki* and *gyros*, a favorite for many!

FOOTSTEPS THROUGH ATHINA

GREEK CUISINE

Since Greece is a sea country and no part of the land is more than 90 miles from the sea, there is an abundance of fresh *psari*, fish and *thalassina*, seafood. Fish and seafood from the Mediterranean is much tastier than that from the ocean and very popular in Greece. Be sure to check out fish and seafood tavernas that serve the very finest!

There are many traditional Greek combination dishes that you must also try. *Mousaka* (meat and eggplant casserole with béchamel sauce on top), *pastitchio* (Greek lasagna), *dolmades* (grape leaves stuffed with rice and meat), *keftedes* (meatballs) and *yemista* (stuffed tomatoes or peppers) are among the many!

You will notice many Greek appetizers, such as *tiropites*, cheese pies and *spanakopites*, spinach pies; main dishes and desserts that are made with *phyllo* (in Greek this means leaf), paper thin sheets of dough similar to puffed pastry. Phyllo dough is made with flour, water and a small amount of oil. It becomes crispy when baked. Although phyllo dough is available ready made, most Greeks prefer using homemade, for it is much tastier.

You can't come to Greece without trying *souvlaki* (shish kebab) or *gyros* (shaved slices of pork or beef) wrapped in *pita* bread (round flatbread) and served with delicious *tzatziki*  sauce (made from yogurt and cucumbers). The taste is exquisite and I guarantee you that you will never find it this tasty back home. There are several great souvlaki places in Monasteraki.

After you are finished eating your main course, do try some Greek desserts. Although most Greek people usually prefer fruit over dessert right after a meal, there are several traditional desserts that you can order at any restaurant. The most popular ones are *kataifi* (shredded wheat, nuts with phyllo dough), *baklavas* (nuts and phyllo) and *galatobouriko* (custard with phyllo). These are sprinkled with syrup made from honey or sugar with water. They are

FOOTSTEPS THROUGH ATHINA

very sweet and usually served in smaller portions. You might even be able to find *loukoumades*, deep fried dough balls coated with sugar, syrup or honey and sprinkled with cinnamon. They are mouthwatering delicious!

Now that you have learned all about the Greek cuisine you are probably ready to venture off to try some of these dishes. But first you need to know a bit about the eating patterns of the Greek people which are a bit different than what you are accustomed to back home. Greeks usually do not have a big breakfast; most will settle for a coffee and a piece of bread with either cheese or honey. Children love cereal, as do kids back home. If you are staying at a hotel, chances are you will be able to choose a number of things to eat from an international buffet table. Lunch in Greece is usually served between 12 and 3. It may consist of a simple, small meal; however, some people prefer to eat a big meal at this time. There are still quite a few people who like to have a big lunch (comparable to our dinners) and even indulge in an afternoon *siesta* for a few hours following the meal. Dinner in Greece is served at a much later time, especially in the summer. Many people go out at about 9 or 10 o'clock. As with lunch, dinner may consist of a small or large meal. There is no need to worry about this when eating in restaurants since people tend to order a big meal, usually consisting of multiple appetizer dishes.

One very important thing to know about eating out in Greece is that not only do Greeks take pride in their wonderful cuisine, they often value eating and enjoying their food in the company of others. When you go out to eat with Greeks, they never are in a hurry to eat and run. They love to sit around for hours engaging in conversation and having a good time. In fact, in most Greek restaurants the waiter likes to leave the people alone to enjoy their meal. It is not a sign of bad service - this is part of Greek culture - eating, drinking and enjoying the moment with good company.

SHOPPING IN ATHENS

Although shopping is usually not the number one priority for visitors to Athens who are busy visiting all the magnificent sites, it can certainly be a real treat for shopaholics and tourists. If you like to shop, you are really in luck because within the last two decades fabulous malls have popped up all over the place. In fact, shopping therapy tends to be a very popular pastime of the Athenians. Once you check out the fabulous malls, specialty shops and boutiques that are spread throughout Athens and its neighboring suburbs, you will understand why. Shopping is certainly one of my main pleasures while I am there! So come with me as our footsteps soar through shopping paradise and I introduce you to several of my favorite places!

GREAT SHOPPING AREAS

<u>Athens</u>: You can find a number of great shopping areas in downtown Athens. Check out the sections of this book that take you along Ermou, Stadiou, Panepistimiou (Attica Department Store) and Akademia Streets, and through the area of Monasteraki  (souvenir shops) and the nearby district of Kolonaki. All these areas have many specialty shops, department stores and boutiques.

<u>Halandri</u>: I may be a bit biased here since this is my neighborhood; where I lived for a number of years and always stay when I return back home. Halandri is a Northern suburb that is quite renowned for its fabulous shopping centers and stores. It is

FOOTSTEPS THROUGH ATHINA

SHOPPING IN ATHENS

a beautiful suburb, and if you get a chance to visit it, you will be impressed with its scores of stores, malls and eating establishments located in the downtown area.

The Mall is located near the Athens Olympic Stadium in the northern suburb of Maroussi. It is the biggest mall in Greece and quite phenomenal! The mall has approximately 200 of the most renowned Greek & international retail stores. Among my very favorites are Zara, Mango, Sfera and Koton. You can certainly shop till you drop! And if you get tired, you can go see a movie at one of the 15 screen multiplex cinema or grab a bite to eat on the top floor of the mall. There you will find a food court with

over 25 restaurants and fast food chains offering exquisite traditional and international food. The restaurants are enclosed under a glass roof. There is even a huge terrace where you can enjoy the breathtaking view of the Olympic Stadium and surrounding Athens.

After I have indulged in hours of shopping, I like to take a break at the souvlaki Restaurant called Psitopoleio Ladi & Rigani (The Oil & Oregano Grill). The authentic souvlaki and Greek style French fries are the best and certainly help recharge your batteries for more shopping! Oh, one more thing about The Mall; it has very good public access. The Neratziotissa Train Station has a stop right below it. If you are coming by car, you can take the Attiki Odos Motorway.

Hours: Monday - Friday: 9:00 am – 9:00 pm
Saturday: 9:00 am – 8:00 pm
Sunday: Mall is closed but Restaurants, Cafes, & Cinemas are open.

FOOTSTEPS THROUGH ATHINA

Kifissia: This is one of the most prestigious and oldest northern suburbs in Athens. It is a posh area with beautiful villas, gardens and trees. It has numerous fashionable shopping malls, Cinemax Cinemas, the Kifissia Bowling Center and many smaller designer shops and chic restaurants.

Glyfada: An upscale suburb southeast of Athens and the largest city in the southern suburbs. Its prime waterfront location, rich commercial center, modern business center, luxurious seaside hotels, beautiful villas and developed transportation network have contributed to making it the Riviera of the East.

GREEK DESIGNERS

The Greek historian Herodotus, who lived in the 5th century BC and is considered the "Father of History", wrote about the significance of fashion and accessories in antiquity. Archeological findings have also confirmed the value and beauty of such items. Fashion in today's Greece is still of utmost importance and we see quite often that the styles reflect the ancient Greek traditions. Greece has a number of renowned fashion designers, many who have won international recognition for their men's and women's collections. Among those are Sophia Kokosalaki - a London based designer known for her classic Grecian style, knitwear and leather; John Varvatos - a Greek American contemporary menswear fashion designer; Michael Aslanis - known for his fabulous women's and men's line; Elina Lembessi - whose fashions include attractive, pretty creations; Yiorgos Eleftheriades - who is known for his impeccable tailoring on quality fabrics for men and women's fashion; and Chara Lembessi, Deux Hommes, Dimitris Alexakis & Grigoris Triantafyllou, Angelos Bratis and Vasso Consola, among others.

Footsteps Through Athina

Specialty Shops & Boutiques

Until the development of department stores and malls, small shops and boutiques were basically the place where all Greeks shopped. They still are quite popular today and in addition to Greek and International chain stores, you will find many local specialized shops throughout the country. One main difference with stores in Greece and back home is that they only have sales twice a year: January-February and July-August. Store hours in Greece generally are: Monday, Wednesday and Saturday - 8:30 am to 3:00 pm and Tuesday, Thursday and Friday - 8:30 to 2:00 pm and 5:00 pm to 8:00 pm. Large department stores are usually open: Monday to Friday - 8:30 am to 8:00 pm and Saturdays - 8:30 am to 3:00 pm. Malls often have different hours.

Traveling Salesmen

During the 60's the *dosas*, traveling salesman, was very popular in Greece and the rest of Europe. He would go door to door selling clothing, housewares, bedding, jewelry and numerous other items. He would return on a weekly or monthly basis to collect his payment. Although this is no longer a common practice, you will often see small trucks traveling around the neighborhoods in which the driver (often times a gypsy) uses a microphone to announce all his products - which are usually fruit and vegetables. There is a scale hanging from the side of the truck to weigh the items to determine the cost. The produce is usually of very good quality and Greeks tend to take advantage of this opportunity when the truck appears on their street.

FOOTSTEPS THROUGH ATHINA

OUTDOOR MARKETS

The *laiki agora*, outdoor street market, is similar to our farmers market back home but offers so much more! Such markets are very popular, for they carry the finest, freshest produce at prices that can't be beat. They additionally sell household items, dry goods, dried herbs and spices, Greek CD's, clothing, shoes and costume jewelry. I have picked up some great gifts at the neighborhood markets. As you walk around, you will hear vendors shouting and competing with each other and insisting that their products are the best. Several of them speak English, so don't be afraid to ask questions. Most of the markets also have a snack area where you can eat fresh *souvlaki*. Such markets appear once per week in many Athenian neighborhoods and usually run from 7 am to 2 pm. It is a real treat visiting the *laiki* and I highly recommend you go if the opportunity arises. It is truly a cultural experience.

THE PERIPTERO

You might be wondering what the small, square, shed-like painted box is on central streets and squares throughout Greece. It is called a *periptero* and functions as a sidewalk kiosk; a Greek version of our 7-11 convenience stores. And even if it is small, it sells anything and everything imaginable! The typical *periptero* has an exhaustive list of newspapers, tablets, pens, cigarettes, candy, stamps, bus and train tickets, souvenirs, ice cream, water, soda, books, phone cards for both Greece and other countries and much, much more! If you are having problems finding something you want, just ask; chances are the *periptero* has it! Another advantage, this tiny little box tends to have long opening hours and you can often find one that is open 24 hours a day.

SHOPPING IN ATHENS

227

FOOTSTEPS THROUGH ATHINA

PSILIKATZIDIKO

In addition to the chains of big super markets and the *Periptero* which appears all over the place, every neighborhood has at least one *psilikatziko*, mini market. Since the store is much bigger than the

little *periptero*, it tends to carry a larger quantity of products, especially within the range of food. It too has more flexible hours than the average supermarket. So if you run out of something and need to replace it quickly, take a walk around the neighborhood; chances are you will find a *psilokatziko* nearby.

SUPER MARKETS

Within the last two decades, European supermarket chains have popped up all over Greece. The advantage of being in the European Union has meant that so many products from various countries are now available in Greece and it is no longer necessary to leave the country in search of such items. The selection is incredible! European supermarkets are not only filled with food, but also clothing, house goods, toys, books and so much more. Several of the supermarkets even have restaurants that offer incredible, traditional Greek meals. The most popular chain of Greek supermarkets in Athens include: Alfa-Vita Vasilopoulos, Atlantic, Bazaar, Carrefour, Marinopoulos, Dia, Galaxias, Metro, Proton, Sklaventis, Thanopoulos, Trofino and Veropoulos (Spar franchise). A trip to a Greek supermarket is certainly a cultural experience that should be included in all visitors' itineraries. It is advisable to go during the weekdays, as both evenings and weekends tend to be very crowded. Oh, and something to point out - if you intend to use a shopping cart (that is usually located in the parking lot or at the front of the store), you will need

Footsteps Through Athina

to insert a Euro coin in the lock to release the cart. Once you return the cart and insert the cable, the coin will be returned.

Bookstores

If you are tired of sightseeing and sunbathing and need to read a good book, then you are in luck, for Athens has several wonderful bookstores spread throughout the city and suburbs. Among the most popular are Eleutheroudakis and Papasotiriou with a fine selection of English books and great cafés where you can read and relax over a snack and drink.

Ikea

In April 2004, the Swedish furniture store Ikea opened in Spata Greece. Located at the outside edge of Eleftherios Venizelos Airport, this store has become a favorite among the Athenians. In fact, if you plan on visiting, try to avoid going on weekends! Although the majority of products are the same as what you can find back home, it is still a cultural experience going to a store in another country.

Jewelry

Jewelry making has been a tradition of Greece since antiquity and today the Greeks hold the front rank among goldsmiths for their superb quality of workmanship. You will be amazed at how many jewelry shops appear in Athens, especially around the Plaka area. There you can find unique, traditional pieces of silver and gold adorned with Minoan, Archaic and Byzantine designs that reflect the Greek heritage and culture. For years, Greek jewelers such as Lalaounis and Zolatas have become internationally famous. Today, a number of contemporary designers, such as Elena Votsi

Footsteps Through Athina

(who designed the Olympic Medal), Lina Fanourakis, and Mariana Petridi are among the many popular names representing Greek jewelry. A great store to visit is Folli Follie that was founded by Dimitris Koutsolioutsos in 1986. Branches appear all over Greece and also in 24 countries throughout the world. You can pick up a lot of fun jewelry at this store.

Shoe Stores

It won't take long before noticing that Greeks of all ages walk around everywhere in gorgeous *papoutsia*, shoes! This is another tradition that dates back to in ancient Greece. Shoes and sandals were of great importance in antiquity and aristocratic women owned at least twenty pairs of shoes. They would employ slaves solely to carry around their supply of shoes when they left home. Greek shoes are of the finest quality and design. You will find great shoe stores throughout all of Athens. Some of the prominent Greek designers are: Bournazos, Kalogirou, Mouriadis, Moschoutis and Petrides. For the younger group, many of the international shoe stores such as Adidas, Clarks, Diesel, Foot Locker, New Balance, Nine West and Timberland can be found in several shopping centers. Should your feet get tired with your footsteps through Athens, stop at the Stavros Melissinos Shop (2 Agias Theklas Street) in Monasteraki and pick out a pair of great Greek sandals. Following his father's footsteps, the poet/sandal maker has designed sandals for very famous people such as Sophia Loren, Jacqueline Onassis, Anthony Quinn, Gary Cooper, queen Sofia of Spain, the Beatles and many other stars and dignitaries. All of his sandals are based on the footwear of the Ancient Greeks.

FOOTSTEPS THROUGH ATHINA

SPICE SHOPS

If you want to bring home the delicious, aromatic flavor of herbs and spices used in Greek cooking, you can pick up some up at the outdoor markets, supermarkets, shops at Monasteraki and specialized herb stores such as Elixir (Evripidou 41), Bachar (Evripidou 31), and Thiamis (Asklipiou 71).

SOUVENIRS

Greek souvenirs can be found in many places throughout Athens such as the *periptero*, department stores, and museum shops. However, for the best selection and price (remember you can bargain here), visit the area of Monastiraki with its narrow streets filled with numerous tourist stores selling Greek artifacts.

MUSIC STORES

Don't forget to bring home the sound of Greek music and play it as you are looking through your photos and indulging in a Greek meal smothered with herbs and spices. The dynamic, vigorous rhythm, along with all your great memories will make you feel as if your footsteps are still traveling through Athina. You can find a wide selection of Greek CD's (and international, too) at several places: stores in Monastiraki, Metropolis Music Store (66 Panepistimiou), Virgin Megastore (7 Stadiou) and Eleftheroudakis Bookstores.

SHOPPING IN ATHENS

231

SHOPPING IN ATHENS

FOOTSTEPS THROUGH ATHINA

 HELPFUL GREEK WORDS

Το Εμπορικό Κέντρο • To Emboree<u>ko</u> <u>Ken</u>tro • Shopping Mall
Το Πολυκαστάστημα • To Poleeka<u>ta</u>steema • Department Store
Η Λαϊκή Αγορά • Ee Laee<u>kee</u> A<u>gora</u> • Farmer's Market
Το Περίπτερο • To Pe<u>ree</u>ptero • Kiosk
Το Ψιλικατζίδικο • To Pseeleeka<u>tzee</u>deeko • Mini Super Market
Το βιβλιοπωλείο • To Veevleeopo<u>lee</u>o • Bookstore
Τα Μαγαζιά Μπαχαρικών • Ta Maga<u>zya</u> Baharee<u>kon</u> • Spice Shops
Το κοσμηματοπωλείο • To Kosmeematopo<u>lee</u>o • Jewelry Shop

FOOTSTEPS THROUGH ATHINA

SPORTS AND LEISURE

Since antiquity, sports have been a significant and vital part of Greek life. The Ancient Greeks considered sports to be an integral part of a child's education that cultivated both the body and mind. Men and boys practiced sports every day in order to stay fit. The Greeks were very big sports fans and as you know, Greece is the country where the Olympic Games originated.

Today, sports are still highly valued in Greek society. During the past few decades, Greece has organized numerous sporting events, including the fabulous Athens 2004 Olympic Games. These events have contributed to the construction of many modern facilities throughout Athens and the rest of the country, and have also given the Greeks the opportunity to participate in their favorite sports. When visiting Greece, you can attend several exciting sports events and find facilities to practice your favorite sport. Some exciting events to attend are:

ATHENS MARATHON: This event commemorates the famous 42 kilometer race of the soldier and ancient Greek hero, Pheidippides, that took place in 490 BC. It begins at the town of Marathon and ends in the famous Panathenaic (Kalimarmaro) Stadium in Athens. Since the revival of the Olympic Games in 1896, the modern Marathon was re-established and now takes place annually on the first Sunday of November.

ATHENS SPATATHION: This event is an ultra-distance foot race that occurs every year on the last Friday of September.

ACROPOLIS RALLY OF GREECE: Originating in 1926, the Acropolis Rally is still thriving today. Every June, top rally drivers from all over the world come to Athens to participate in this exciting event.

FOOTSTEPS THROUGH ATHINA

SPORTS IN GREECE

FOOTBALL: In Greece and many other countries of the world, football (soccer) is considered to be the national and favorite sport of the country. Although Athens has many football teams, there are two major ones: Panathinaikos (Olympic Stadium of Maroussi) and Olympiakos (Georgios Karaiskaiki Stadium in Piraeus). Football games are played on Saturdays and Sundays from September to May. Greeks have a devotion to soccer and during the season they gather in cafés and restaurants to watch these games. As you can imagine, the passionate fans get very loud and emotional over the outcomes of this sport.

GOLF: Although golf is not as popular of a sport in Greece as it is in the States, the Greeks are very proud of their international golf course in Glyfada. The Glyfada Golf Course features a pro shop, a practice range, dressing rooms, a golf academy, restaurants, a clubhouse, a bar, two tennis courts and a convention room.

HORSE RACES: The Markopoulo racetrack is located in Spata, near the airport. Races take place on Monday, Wednesday and Friday at 5:00 pm in the summer and 3:00 pm in winter.

CYCLING: Since many streets have recently been banned to traffic cycling has become more popular among the Athenians. There are several agencies that rent out city, trekking and mountain bikes and also organize bike tours. Several of these agencies will deliver the bicycle to your hotel.

FOOTSTEPS THROUGH ATHINA

WATER ACTIVITIES

You can't come to Athens without visiting the Greek *paralia*, beach. Especially after days of walking along the sites, there is nothing more calming and relaxing than strolling along the sandy and pebble beaches of Attica with  the sun beating down upon the majestic landscapes, shorelines and amazing crystal-clear, turquoise water. No picture could ever do justice to such beauty nor recapture the sensation of such moments!

There are several excellent and picturesque beaches along the coastal neighborhoods of Athens, which is often called the Athens Riviera, the Gold Coast or even the Apollo Coast. The majority of beaches found here are National Tourist Organization of Greece's public beaches (also referred to as state public beaches) in which you pay a very small or moderate entrance fee (4-12 Euros).  These beaches not only provide swimming in quality water, several of them also offer a number of amenities such as dressing rooms, showers, restrooms, umbrellas, lounge chairs, snack bars, restaurants and life guards. At most of the state public beaches, you will have the opportunity to windsurf and also take lessons from a qualified staff member. A number also offer canoes, *pedalos* (paddle boats), tennis, volleyball, basketball courts and playgrounds. Some free beaches (especially those without gates) often have umbrellas and chairs that are brought in by an outside person who will charge you about 3-4 Euros to use during your stay.

Private beaches are accessible for a higher fee and some tend to be quite expensive. In addition to providing the facilities that public beaches offer, these beaches offer much more such as waterslides, canoeing, waterskiing and windsurfing. Let's take a look at the coastal beaches around Athens.

Footsteps Through Athina

Beaches Around Athens

Agia Marina Beach - Porto Rafti: (30 km from center): Although this is not a state public beach, it is very picturesque and sandy. There are several restaurants and tavernas within the area. Accessible via Ktel bus.

Agion Apostolon Beach - Oropos: (50 km from center): Located in Oropos, this is a state public beach with pebbles and clean water. Accessible via Ktel bus.

Agios Kosmas Beach: (14 km from center): This state public beach is very near the city making it a popular destination. It provides umbrellas, lounge chairs and numerous other services. Accessible via tram.

Agios Nikolaos Artemidos Beach - Loutsa: (32 km from center): Although Agios Nikolaos is not on the list of state public beaches, it's a very popular and beautiful beach with a snack bar. It also provides surfboard rentals and windsurfing. The area is a great place to visit at night as it offers several fish tavernas, bars and cafés.

Alimos: (8 km from center): Alimos Beach is the nearest beach to center of Athens. During the weekday, the lounge chairs are free but during the weekend a charge of 7 Euro applies. Since it is so close to the center, this beach is usually very crowded. Accessible via tram.

Alipedou Voulas A & B: (17 km from center): Due to its proximity, beauty of these beaches and numerous services offered, both are quite popular among Athenians and tourists. You will find a water slide, bar, restaurant, changing rooms, beach and volleyball courts and a long stretch of a sandy beach at each. Voula Beach A was awarded the Blue Flag by the European Union for meeting the strict criteria of cleanliness and organization.

Anavyssos Beach: (45 km): Situated in Anavyssos, in front of the Eden hotel, this is a state public beach providing windsurfing and many other activities.

Asteria Sea Side Beach – Glyfada: (20 km from center): The close

proximity of this beach to the center of Athens has always made this a very popular beach. Quite recently the state operated beach has undergone a total transformation turning it into an awesome, upscale spot on the Athenian Riviera. It has a fabulous sandy beach, private bungalows surrounded by landscaped grounds and provides a number of fine amenities. These include: lounge chairs, umbrellas, swimming pools, lockers, changing rooms, showers, trampolines, a playground, a water park, a restaurant, three bars, a sea park, volleyball and football courts and water volleyball.

Astir Palace Beach – Vouliagmeni: (20 km from center): This is one of the most favorite beaches for all. It is beautiful and offers so much: water and jet skiing, sailing and windsurfing. There is a first aid station on the premises and also a *periptero* that sells a large variety of Greek and international newspapers and magazines. It is one of the most expensive beach in the area.

Attica Coast – Vouliagmeni: (15 km from center): This attractive, state public beach offers a restaurant, snack bar, cafés and a number of sports facilities. Accessible via Buses 114, 116, 340, E22.

Avlaki Beach – Porto Rafti: (30 km from center): This state public beach provides umbrellas, lounge chairs, a basketball court and a snack bar. There are many fine restaurants, tavernas and fast food establishments in the area. Accessible via Ktel bus.

Footsteps Through Athina

Cape Sounion: (68 km southeast from the center): The site of the Temple of Poseidon has a sandy beach with nearby tavernas and cafés.

Edem Beach - Paleo Faliro: (6 km from center): The location of this beach is great; however, this makes it extremely crowded. Since it is publicly managed, there is no entrance fee. The down-the-road Poseidon Hotel offers private beach facilities and operates a nearby taverna. There is also an Edem Taverna close to the beach catering to hungry beachgoers.

Erotospila Beach - Porto Rafti: (30 km from center): Although this is not a state public beach, it attracts people on the weekends. It is a small sandy bay with caves. It has a snack bar on its premises. You can arrive here with the Ktel bus.

Kakia Thalassa Beach - Keratea: (41 km from center): This state public beach provides lounge chairs, umbrellas, changing rooms, showers and a restaurant. There are fish tavernas in the nearby area. Accessible via Ktel bus service.

Kalamos Beach: (30 km from center): Although this quiet beach is less frequented by visitors, the sea is clean and the beach is sandy. There is no entrance fee. There are a number of restaurants and tavernas in the area. Accessible via Ktel bus.

Kavouri Beaches: (10 km from center): The beaches in this picturesque area offer free access and gather large crowds of people. There are several gulfs that are ideal for swimming. The surrounding area is filled with many cafés, snack booths and restaurants. Accessible via Bus A1, E1, E1, E19, E29, 114, 115, 116, 138, 149, 162, 163.

Kokkino Limanaki: (26 km southeast of center): This is not a state public beach; however, it attracts many for its sandy beach and the blue green water of the sea. There is a camping site in the area. It can be reached by taking the Ktel bus.

FOOTSTEPS THROUGH ATHINA

Lagonissi Beach: (35 km from center): This luxurious beach is part of the Grand Resort Lagonissi Hotel and is quite expensive. The beach provides many amenities such as: a floating bar, Thai & Shiatsu massage, body painting, sun beds, a restaurant that delivers food to your lounge chair, volleyball, parasailing, water skiing and banana tubes. It has been awarded the European Union Blue Flag for excellence. Accessible via Ktel bus.

Legrenon Beach: (60 km from center): Although this sandy beach located near Sounion is not a state public beach, it is very popular. There are tavernas nearby. It is serviced by the Ktel bus.

Marikes Beach - Rafina: (32 km from center): Located within the vicinity of Rafina; except for a snack bar and a volleyball court, this sandy beach offers very few facilities. The area is serviced by the Ktel bus.

Mati Beach - Nea Makri: (25 km from center): Mati Beach is a sandy beach that is quite popular in Nea Makri. There is no entrance fee to swim here. It can be reached by the Ktel bus.

Nea Makri Beach: (25 km from center): The Nea Makri Beach is a state public beach that provides umbrellas, lounge chairs, showers and swimming platforms. The Ktel bus operates services to this area.

Nea Palatia Beach - Oropos: (50 km from center): Located in Oropos, this pebbled beach is not on the list of EOT. You may visit it using the Ktel bus.

Porto Germanos Beaches: (71 km from center). The area of Porto Germanos is filled with long stretches of clean, sandy and pebbled beaches. These beaches attract many people. You can find water sports facilities at a number

Footsteps Through Athina

of them. The town of Porto Germanos is filled with excellent fish tavernas. Accessible via Ktel bus.

Psatha Beach: (66 km from center): This beach is in the vicinity before Porto Germanos. It is not a state public beach. Accessible via Ktel Bus.

Schinias - Karavi Beach: (45 km northeast from center and on the southeast side of Marathon): This is a favorite among windsurfers since the beach is long and located in a windy area. It is a state public beach providing umbrellas, lounge chairs, snack bars, restaurants, football and volleyball courts and on certain days, bungee jumping. Accessible by Ktel bus.

Varkiza Beach: (27 km southeast of center) is full of activities such as tennis and volleyball courts, windsurfing, a play area for children, water slides, individual cabins, snack bars, a first aid center, and a lifeguard unit. Since it is a bit far from the city, it tends to be the less crowded. Accessible via Bus 115, 116, 125, 340, 171.

Vouliagmeni Beach: (23 km southeast of center) also offers tennis and volleyball courts in addition to water slides, snack bars and a play area for children.

Vouliagmeni Lake: (12 km from center): This enchanting, small lake is located south of the town of Vouliagmeni. It has fresh water that is fed by underground currents through the mass of Mount Hymettus. The water maintains a constant 24° Celsius temperature and functions as a year-round spa, as it has therapeutic values due to the minerals in the water. The facility is equipped with umbrellas and lounge chairs, a café and a hydrotherapy unit. Accessible via Buses 114,116, G1, E22.

Zoumberi Beach - Nea Makri: (35 km from center). This beach is very popular, as it provides a football and volleyball court and also scuba diving. There are several fish tavernas in the area. Accessible via Ktel bus.

Footsteps Through Athina

Amusement Parks

Allou Fun Park
Odos: Kifisou Avenue & Ralli Petrou Street
       Agios Ioannis Rentis
Hours: Daily: 5:00 pm - 1:00 am
       Friday: 5:00 pm - 2:00 am
       Saturday: 10:00 am - 2:00 am
       Sunday: 10:00 am - 1:00 am

Allou Fun Park is the only amusement park in Greece that has  something for people of all ages, even though it isn't quite geared towards very young children. Located next to the multiplex Village Park in Agios Ioannis Rentis, the Fun Park opened in October 2002. Although Allou (meaning "somewhere else") is not as large as Disneyland and other thematic parks in the world, it has attracted more than 2 million people. Many of the events change three times a year. The park stays open past midnight throughout the entire week. If you have a chance to visit Allou, I guarantee that you will have a fun time!

Kidom Luna Park
Odos: Kifisou Avenue & Ralli Petrou Street, Agios Ioannis Rentis
Hours: Opened Daily: 5:00 pm - 12:00 am
       Saturday - Sunday: 10:00 am - 12:00 am

Kidom Luna (meaning Moon) Park is next to Allou Fun Park and caters to young children ages 6-12 years old. It has seventeen rides, such as the Mini Big Apple Train, a pirate ship and more!

Fantasy Land
Odos: 46 Kifisias Avenue - Maroussi
Hours: Daily: 5:00 pm - 12:00 midnight
       Saturday - Sunday 10:00 am - 12:00 midnight

Fantasy Land is the biggest Luna park in Athens. It has 11 rides; 1 kiddy ride, 50 games, a 20 meter Ferris wheel, a powerful free-fall, a dragon and a ghost train.

Sports and Leisure

Footsteps Through Athina

Indoor Play Centers

Balloons
Odos: 49 Geor. Papandreou - Zografou
Odos: 243 Kifisias Avenue

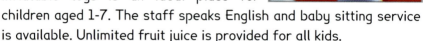

This play center filled with inflatable toys is an ideal place for children aged 1-7. The staff speaks English and baby sitting service is available. Unlimited fruit juice is provided for all kids.

Paramythi
Odos: 25B Ifigeneias Street - Nea Ionia
Hours: Mon - Fri: 10:00 am - 2:00 pm & 5:00 pm - 10:00 pm
Saturday: 10:00 am - 11:00 pm
Sunday: 10:00 am - 10:00 pm

Paramythi is a fun place for children. The play center has slides, bouncing frames, a three story castle with ropes and tunnels, plus much more. Parents can sit at the snack bar that is located next to the entrance.

Renti Family Park
Odos: Petrou Rallis & Thivon Street - Agios Ioannis Rentis
Hours: Daily: 7:00 pm - 1:00 am

Children can play (under the supervision of the staff) on the inflated climbing toys while parents are watching a movie at one of the center's 20 theatres. At 11 pm, parents are allowed to join in the play with their children.

HELPFUL GREEK WORDS

Ο Μαραθώνας • O Marathonas • Marathon
Το ποδόσφαιρο • To Podosfero • Football (Soccer)
Οι ιπποδρομίες • Ee Ipodromeees • Horse races
Το ποδήδαλτο • To Podeelato • Bicycle
Η παραλία • Ee Paraleea • Beach
Το Λούνα Παρκ • To Louna Park • Amusement Park

FOOTSTEPS THROUGH ATHINA

PRACTICAL INFORMATION

GETTING TO GREECE

If you live in the Americas, the only way to get to Greece is via airplane. There are a few direct flights from New York's Kennedy Airport with the Greek carrier Olympic Airways, Continental Airlines, and Delta Airlines. You can also leave from Atlanta on Delta Airlines, or from Pittsburgh on US Airways. From Canada, Olympic Airways and Air Canada provide direct flights from both Toronto and Montreal. Your other alternative is to leave on a European airline and take a connecting flight to Athens from the country of the carrier. Air France, Alitalia, Lufthansa, British Airways, KLM and Iberia are among those that offer daily flights.

It is much easier for a European visitor to get to Greece since all major European airlines offer a number of daily flights to Athens. Many people opt to drive through Italy to board a ferry boat that connects Italy with the west coast ports of Greece. Boats leave from Ancona, Bari, and Brindisi, Italy, and arrive in Igoumenitsa, Corfu, and Patra, Greece. The one-day trip is quite enjoyable. For an additional fee, you can transport your car and also get a room with a bed. The Euro train and bus are two other options.

ELEFTHERIOS VENIZELOS AIRPORT

The new Eleftherios Venizelos International Airport that opened in 2001 is considered to be one of Europe's best. It is located in Spata, Greece, about 40 minutes from the center of Athens. The airport is named after Eleftherios Venizelos, the Cretan politician and Prime Minister of Greece who played an important role in Crete's autonomy from the Ottoman Turks. The

243

Footsteps Through Athina

state-of-the-art airport is known for its high tech facilities and security systems. It has both short and long-term parking lots. From the connecting Metro train station you can take a train to the center of the city (stops at Syntagma and Monastiraki) in about 44 minutes. Trains run every 30 minutes. A one-way ticket costs about 6 Euros and a round trip 10. You can also take an express bus or taxi to your destination.

When leaving Greece, try to get to the airport early as there are many things to see and do before you depart. First stop should probably be the shopping center that has been ranked among the top finest in European airports. It includes over 50 Greek and international stores selling designer name clothing, jewelry, CD's, Greek and English books, food products from Greece and so much more. A great opportunity to pick up last minute gifts and souvenirs! If you want to indulge in one last Greek meal, stop at one of the main restaurants or fast food establishments. Younger children can play in the entertainment area. And if you still have a desire to see more antiquity, here's your chance to visit one more museum! Yes believe it or not, just as there are museums in the Metro stations, there is also one here at the airport that displays all the fabulous ancient discoveries that were found around this site.

Getting Around Athens

THE METRO LINES

As previously mentioned, the new Athens Metro is a unique monumental achievement. The Metro provides impeccable service and also serves as an ancient and contemporary art museums that expose daily commuters to the world of Greek art that would have remained unknown to so many, had they not been showcased through this underground network. Twenty-three Athenian stations, with spotless marble walls and granite floors are home to these

FOOTSTEPS THROUGH ATHINA

treasures. They are protected by modern security systems, policemen and a qualified staff and, oddly enough, all Greeks adhere to the no smoking regulations.

The Metro currently has three lines and extensions, and work still continues. Line 1 (the green line) is the oldest line and runs from the suburb of Kifissia to the seaport of Piraeus; Line 2 (red line) from Agios Andonios to Agios Dimitrios (Al Panagoulis) and Line 3 (blue line) from Doukissis Plakendias to Egaleo. Doukissis Plakendias is also where the Metro connects with the Suburban Train (see description below) from the airport. The Metro trains are very fast, running every three minutes during rush hour and the rest of the day every 10 minutes.

Tickets can be purchased at any Metro Station. The cost is 0.80 Euro for a one way ticket and 0.40 Euro for a student. You must validate the ticket at an automated machine before entering the train. Tickets are valid for 90 minutes from the time they are stamped. Metro tickets can also be used for connections on buses, trolleys, tram and part of the suburban railway. Daily tickets can be purchased for 3 Euros and weekly ones for 10 Euros. If you fail to validate your ticket, you will be fined 60 times the original cost. Do be careful; the tickets are frequently checked and controlled! The Metro stations close at midnight and reopen at 5am.

PROASTIAKOS · TRAIN

The Proastiakos (Suburban Train) is the express suburban railway network of Athens connecting the Larissa Station (Athens Central Railway Station) with the Eleftherios International Airport and Corinth. The suburban railway also connects with the urban Metro trains at a number of stations. They are: Piraeus Line 1; Athens Larissa Station Line 2; Nerantziotissa Line 1; Plakentias Line 3; Pallini Line 3; Paiania Kantza Line 3; Koropi Line 3; and the Airport Line 3. The ticket fares range up to 6 Euros depending on destination.

Footsteps Through Athina

BUSES & TROLLEYS IN ATHENS

Athens has a very modern and efficient bus network and also holds the European record for the number of environmental buses that run on natural gas. The blue city buses and yellow trolleys take you anywhere you want to go. Buses leave every ten to thirty minutes from two main stations. Those going to the seaside leave from the Akadimia bus station while north suburban buses leave from Kaningos Square. Most are also equipped with screens and audio announcements in both Greek and English.

A one-way bus or trolley ticket costs 0.80 Euros and can be purchased at all Metro stations and at most periptero kiosks. Booklets of ten tickets are available for frequent travelers. Tickets must be validated in one of the machines on the bus. If your ticket is not validated and you get checked, you will be fined 60 times the cost of the ticket. Buses and trolleys run from about 5am until 11pm or midnight.

THE ATHENS COASTAL TRAM

After 44 years of absence, trams officially returned to Athens. The sleek, new, high-tech trams run on tracks that begin in Syntagma and end at the seaside suburbs of Glyfada, Faliro and Voula. Although the trams go very slow (it takes an hour to arrive in Glyfada), the carriages are air conditioned and quite comfortable. They also take you down residential streets in old neighborhoods that regular buses don't, giving you an opportunity to see a different view of Athens. Trams run from 5am to 1am from Monday to Thursday and Sunday, and around-the-clock on Fridays and Saturdays. The average waiting time is 7-8 minutes (between 5am to 10pm); 10 minutes (between

10pm to 1am) and 40 minutes (between 1am to 5am). A single fare ticket costs 0.60 Euro.

KTEL BUSES

If you want to travel outside of Athens via bus, you will most likely go with a KTEL bus. These buses are very clean, comfortable and air conditioned. There are four KTEL bus terminals in Athens serving East Attica, West Attica, the Peloponnese, and Delphi & Northern Greece. Buses that go to Marathon, Oropos, Lavrio, Sounion, and Rafina can be located in front of the Ethniki Amina Metro Station or in front of the bus stops that have an orange sign. You can purchase a ticket on board that does not need to be validated. Prices vary according to your destination.

TAXIS

It is very common and inexpensive to take a taxi in Athens. These yellow automobiles are all over the place. In fact, there are about 15,000 of them in Athens. If you need a taxi, you can either hail one down by waving your hand or call a taxi company to be picked up - there will be an additional fee for this. It is common practice for the taxi driver to stop and pick up others while you are in the car; however, he needs to first ask your permission. The majority of taxi drivers all speak English so you should have no problem communicating. And ever since the Athens 2004 Olympics, most taxi drivers are very polite, kind and careful about keeping their taxi in tiptop shape. By law, all taxis must use a meter to bring you to your destination. There are two tariffs. No. 1 tariff is used for the day rate (5am to midnight). After midnight, tariff 2 is applied. Most taxis also have a GPS system so they shouldn't get lost taking you to your final destination.

FERRIES & FLYING DOLPHINS

Greek ferries are an economical and fun way to get to an island. They are designed with air conditioned rooms that have comfortable

Footsteps Through Athina

seats, tables, TVs and snack bars offering a good variety of food. If you are going to a further away island that requires you to travel overnight, you can reserve a cabin with a bed. The fastest way to travel to the islands is by a hydrofoil flying dolphin, or high speed catamaran. The boats skim above the water and cross inter-island distances in half the time of ferries. Tickets can be purchased ahead of time or shortly before departure at tickets booths in front of the ferries. Keep in mind that on weekends and holidays the tickets go fast and it is advisable to purchase tickets in advance.

If you are planning to travel by boat or ferry, you will need to get to the port of Piraeus. You can reach it by taking the Proastiakos train from Larissa Station, the Metro Line 1 or the 040 bus from Filellinon (next to Syntagma Square). A number of boats for the Cyclades leave from the ports of Rafina & Lavrion. Buses to these ports leave every half hour and can be picked up at the Ethniki Amina Metro Station. It is important that you quickly get on and off the boats as they depart immediately upon arriving at the dock.

SIGHTSEEING BUS #400

Visitors to Athens can take the Sightseeing Bus #400 which makes stops at 20 cultural landmarks. The bus stops are marked with tall blue signs that also indicate the time that the bus will arrive at the stop and a map. Bus tickets cost 5 Euros and can be purchased from the driver. The ticket is good for twenty-four hours. You can hop on and off the buses as often as you like. The buses run every half hour from 7am until 9pm. The sightseeing bus is the perfect solution for escaping the heat on a very hot day.

USEFUL WEBSITES

NOTE: MANY OF THE FOLLOWING ARE IN GREEK, BUT HAVE ENGLISH LINKS

GENERAL INFORMATION ABOUT ATHENS

Athens Attica Greece	www.athensattica.gr
Athens, Greece: City Guide	www.athenscity.gr
Ancient Greece.org	www.ancient-greece.org
Athens Guide	www.greek-islands.us/athens
Athens in Pictures	www.athensinpictures.com
Athens Info Guide	www.athensinfoguide.com
Athens21stCentury	www.athens-today.com
Daily Frappe	www.dailyfrappe.com
Greece-Athens.com Athens City Guide	www.greece-athens.co
Greece Taxiwww.atticadps.gr	www.greecetaxi.gr
Greeka.com	www.greeka.com
Greek landscapes	www.greeklandscapes.com
Hellas Guide	www.hellas-guide.com
Igogreece.com	www.igogreece.com
In2Greece	www.in2greece.com
Magical Journeys	www.magicaljourneys.com
Matt Barrett's Greece Travel Guide	www.greecetravel.com
Odysseus-Hellenic Ministry of Culture	odysseus.culture.gr
Tour Trip Greece	www.tourtripgreece.gr
Travelinfo.gr	www.travelinfo.gr/athens
Travel to Athens. EU	www.traveltoathens.eu
Welcome to Athens	www.akropol.net
Yasou	yasou.org

EMBASSIES

American Embassy	athens.usembassy.gov
Greek Embassy – Washington	www.greekembassy.org

GREEK FOOD

Greek-Recipe.com	www.greek-recipe.com
Ultimate Guide to Greek Food	www.ultimate-guide-to-greek-food.com

USEFUL WEBSITES

MUSEUMS
Atelier Spyros Vassiliou — www.spyrosvassiliou.org
Benaki Museum — www.benaki.gr
Foundation of the Hellenic World — www.fhw.gr
Foundation Melina Mercouri — www.melinamercourifoundation.org.grl
Frissiras Museum — www.frissirasmuseum.com
Greece Museums Guide — www.greece-museums.com
Greek Dances Theatre Dora Stratou — www.grdance.org
Hellenic Society for the Protection of the Environment — www.ellinikietairia.gr
Herakleidon Experience in Visual Arts — www.herakleidon-art.gr
Ilias Lalaounis Jewerly Museum — www.lalaounis-jewelrymuseum.gr
Jewish Museum of Greece — www.jewishmuseum.gr
Museum of Cycladic Art — www.cycladic.gr
Museum of Greek Children's Art — www.childrensartmuseum.gr
National Archaeological Museum — www.culture.gr/h/1/eh151.jsp?obj_id=3249
National Bank of Greek Cultural Foundation — www.miet.gr
National Gallery Alexandros Soutzos — www.nationalgallery.gr
Philatelic Museum — english.postalmuseum.gr
Theatre Museum — www.theatremuseum.grh
The New Acropolis Museum — www.newacropolismuseum.gr

ORTHODOXY
Orthodox Name Days — www.namedays.gr

SCHOOLS
American Community School of Athens — www.acs.gr
Deree College — www.acg.edu

SHOPPING
Attica Department Store — www.atticadps.gr
The Mall Athens — www.themallathens.gr

TRANSPORTATION
Athens Tram — www.tramsa.gr
Eleftherios Venizelos Airport — www.aia.gr
Athens Metro — www.ametro.gr

INDEX

Academy of Athens	145
Acropolis	33
Acropolis Metro	46
Agoras Square	82
Agrippa Odeon	115
Airport	243
American College of Greece	192
American Community School	191
Amusement Parks	241
Anafoitika	73
Archaeology	29, 63, 107, 124, 172, 160, 164
Ancient Agora	112
Areos Pagos	51
Arsakeio Girls'School	147
Asia Minor Studies Center	93
Athens Central Market	162
Athens City Hall	161
Athens First Cemetery	69
Athens Map	31
Athens Metro	32
Athens Polytechnion	163
Athens University	146
Attica Department Store	150
Beaches	236
Beth Shalom Synagogue	121
Book Arcade	148
Bookstores	148, 149, 229
Boutiques	226
Buele Gate	35
Buses	246
Caryatids	40
Churches:	
Ag. Dinami	97
Ag. Dionysios	144
Ag. Dionysios Areopagitis	141
Ag. Eleftherios	99
Ag. Georgios Karitsis	153
Ag. Sotira Metamorphosis	94
Ag. Theodori	155
Ag. Triada	123
Church of the Archangels	110
Church of the Metamorphosis	77
Holy Apostles	120
Holy Apostles Solaki	116
Holy Trinity Cathedral	172
Kimissi Chrisokastiotissa	79
Metropolitan Cathedral	98
Petraki Monastery	138
St. Anargyri	118
St. Anargyroi	84
St. Anasthassios Athonite	128
St. Anasthassios Koukouris	127
St. Anna	78
St. Catherine	90
St. Dimitrios	89
St. Fotini	67
St. George	44
St. George Lycavittos	140
St. George of the Rock	75
St. George Rizaris	135
St. Irene	102
St. John the Theologian	85
St. Lykodimou	60
St. Marina	53
St. Mary	101
St. Nicholas/Poorhouse	134
St. Nicholas Rangavas	85
St. Paraskevi	156
St. Paul Anglican	61
St. Phillip	112
St. Spirodonas	172
St. Spyridon	80
St. Symeon	75
Tetraconch Megali Panagia	107
Virgin Mary Chrissospliotissa	155
Virgin Mary of Romvi	101
Virgin Mary Queen of All	104
Cine Paris	91
Climate	22
Columns	29
Currency	25

FOOTSTEPS THROUGH ATHINA

INDEX

Deree University	192
Dora Stratou Dancers	54
Dyonysos Theater	43
Eleutheroudakis Bookstore	149
Erechtheion	40
Ermou Street	97, 100
Etz Hayim Synagogue	121
Evzones	58
Ferries	247
Fethiye Djami Mosque	109
Filomousou Square	90
First Municipal School	84
Flea Market	104
Flying Dolphin	247
Gazi	125
Gazi Factory Workshops	125
Glyfada	225
Greek Alphabet	179
Greek Cuisine	219
Greek Culture	195
Greek Dancing	214
Greek Designers	225
Greek Education	189
Greek Flag	216
Greek Holidays	195
Greek Language	179
Greek Music	217
Greek Orthodox Ceremonies	211
Greek Superstitions	207
Greek Symbolic Artifacts	205
Greek Traditions	195
Hadrian, Statue	116
Hadrian's Arch	65
Hadrian's Library	107
Halandri	167, 223
Hellenic Society/Environment	88
Helpful Expressions	181
Hephaestos Temple	114
Herod Atticus Theater	42
Hilton Hotel	137
Ikea	229
Jewelry	229
Keramikos	120
Keramikos Cemetery	122
Kifissia	167, 225
Kioniski	123
Kiosks	227
Klafthmonas Square	154
Kolokotroni Square	152
Kolonaki	140
Kolonaki Square	140
Konstantinos Tsatsos Residence	93
Korais Square	148
Koranic Theological School	110
Kotzia Square	159
Koumoundourou Square	117
KTEL Bus	247
Language	27
Location & Size	21
Lycavittos Hill	139
Lysikrates Monument	89
Makrigianni District	49
Mall, The	224
Melas Mansion	161
Melina Mercouri Foundation	111
Mercouri, Melina	46, 66, 69, 111, 128, 171
Metro Lines	32, 244
Metropolitan Square	98
Mets District	70
Mini-Market	228
Mitropoulos Street	97
Monastiraki	97, 103
Monastiraki Metro	105
Monastiraki Square	103
Mousikis Concert Hall	138
Museums:	
Acropolis	47
Alexandros Soutzos	136
Archaeological Keramikos	124
Archaeological of Piraeus	172
Athens Municipal Gallery	118
Athens University	76
Bathhouse of the Winds	81
Benaki	131
Benaki Islamic Art	119

INDEX

FOOTSTEPS THROUGH ATHINA

Byzantine and Christian	133
Callas, Maria	126
Ceramics	106
City of Athens	153
Cycladic Art	132
Epigraphical	166
Folk Art, Center of	79
Frissiras	92
Ghikas Gallery	132
Goulandris	167
Greek Children's Art	94
Greek Costume, History of	141
Greek Folk Art	93
Hellenic Children's	92
Heraklion Visual Arts	129
Historical Museum of Greece	152
Jewelry	50
Jewish	95
Kanellopoulos	77
Komboloi	205
Melina Mercouri Cultural Ctr.	128
Municipal Gallery of Piraeus	172
Musical Instruments	72
National Archaeological	164
National Art Gallery	136
National Pinakotheki	136
Nautical	171
Numismatic	144
Philatelic	68
Theatre	147
Traditional Pottery	120
Venizelos	137
War Museum	134
Music Stores	231
National Bank of Greece	149
National Gardens	61
National Library	146
National Technical University	163
Nike Temple	37
Nymphs Hill	53
OAKA	175
Old Parliament House	152
Olympian Zeus Temple	66
Olympic Area	65
Olympic Ceremonies	177, 178
Olympic Emblem	174
Olympic Mascots	175
Olympic Torch	174
Olympic Volunteers	176
Olympics	173
Olympics, Athens 2004	173
Omonia	157
Omonia Metro	158
Omonia Square	157
Ophthalmology Eye Clinic	145
Outdoor Markets	104, 227
Panathenaic Stadium	67
Parliament	57
Parthenon	38
Pedestrian Walk	45
Periptero	227
Philoppapou Hill	53
Phyx Hill	52
Pierce College	192
Piraeus	170
Piraeus Metro	172
Plaka	71
Play Centers	241
Population & People	24
Poulopoulos Hat Factory	128
Propyleia	36
Psirri	117
Puppet Theater	88
Religion	27
Religious Artifacts	208
Roman Agora	107
Roman Baths	63
Runner Statue	135
Saint Filothei House	83
School of the Nation Square	135
Shoe Stores	230
Shopping	223
Sightseeing Bus	248
Sound & Light Show	52
Sounion	169
Soutsos-Rallis Residence	149

253

INDEX

Souvenirs	231	Timeline	11
Specialty Shops	226	Tomb of Unknown Soldier	57
Spice Shops	231	Tower of the Winds	109
Sports	233	Tradition Arts Center	91
Spyros Vassilou Atelier	49	Trains	245
Stadiou Street	152	Trams	246
Stoa of Attalos	114	Travelling Salesmen	226
Suburbs	167	Trolleys	246
Subway Map	32	Tsisdarakis Mosque	106
Super Markets	228	University District	143
Syntagma Metro	56	Varvakios	162
Syntagma Square	55	Vasilissis Sophias	131
Taxis	247	Venizelos Park	137
Thission	127	Water Activities	235
Thraysyllos Monument	44	Yellow House	149
Time	23	Zappeion	62

ATHENS 2004

ANOTHER ATHENS HAS ARISEN!

ABOUT THE AUTHOR

Angelyn Balodimas-Bartolomei was born in Chicago to immigrant Greek parents. Her determination to master the Greek language brought her to Greece, where she earned her B.A. in Greek social work and Greek Studies at Deree College in Athens. Angie then entered the Pedagogical Academy of Greece and, upon graduation, returned to the USA to study for an M.A. at Northeastern Illinois University in Linguistics and English as a Second Language (ESL). She then went on for a Ph.D. degree at Loyola University, which she received in 2004 in Educational and Leadership Policy Studies with a concentration in Comparative Education.

Angie has designed numerous curriculum materials for Greek community schools and founded the GSL (Greek as a Second Language) program at St. Haralambos Greek School in Chicago. She has taught ESL to adult immigrants and continues to study languages. Angie was chosen to attend the Athens 2004 Olympics as a volunteer, where she used her command of several languages to assist spectators. Angie is interested in comparative and international studies, Greek studies, and ESL and language studies. She has presented papers at several conferences for organizations such as the Comparative and International Education Society, Greek Teachers Association, Italian Teachers Association, and the Modern Greek Studies Association. She has served on numerous foreign language committees and serves on the education committee at the Hellenic Museum and Cultural Center in Chicago. In conjunction with her doctoral dissertation, Angie has done extensive Greek, Italian and Jewish studies. She is currently researching Greek identity among second, third, and third-plus generation Greek Americans.

Angie currently is Professor in the School of Education at North Park University for ESL Teachers' Endorsement. Recently she began teaching Comparative and International Education for students in the M.A program. Angie is married to Paul, who emigrated from Italy to the United States as a child. Their three grown children were raised learning foreign languages and traveling back to their parents' ancestral lands.